Library of
Davidson College

ACCOUNTING POLICY FORMULATION
THE ROLE OF
CORPORATE MANAGEMENT

LAUREN KELLY-NEWTON
Graduate School of Management
University of California, Los Angeles

ACCOUNTING POLICY FORMULATION THE ROLE OF CORPORATE MANAGEMENT

ADDISON-WESLEY PUBLISHING COMPANY
Reading, Massachusetts • Menlo Park, California
London • Amsterdam • Don Mills, Ontario • Sydney

This book is in the
Addison-Wesley Paperback Series in Accounting

Consulting Editor
William J. Bruns, Jr.

Copyright © 1980 by Addison-Wesley Publishing Company, Inc. Philippines copyright 1980 by Addison-Wesley Publishing Company, Inc.

All rights reserved. No part of this publication may be reproduced, stored in a retrieval system, or transmitted, in any form or by any means, electronic, mechanical, photocopying, recording, or otherwise, without the prior written permission of the publisher. Printed in the United States of America. Published simultaneously in Canada. Library of Congress Catalog Card No. 80-66770.

ISBN 0-201-05291-1
ABCDEFGHIJ-DO-89876543210

EDITOR'S FOREWORD

The environment for accounting has undergone revolutionary changes in the last decade. Demand for accountability by managers of both public and private organizations has risen significantly. Electronic data transmission, storage, and processing and other information technologies have developed to allow accountants to use methods and processes that would have been considered impossible, or uneconomical, just a few years ago. At the same time, new quantitative methods for solving accounting problems have been developed, and the behavioral sciences have suggested that the impact of accounting goes well beyond the systems and reports which are the most visible product of the accountant's work.

The speed with which these developments have occurred has made it difficult for teachers and students of accounting, and for managers and accountants themselves, to keep their knowledge up-to-date. New solutions to problems, and sometimes even new kinds of accounting problems themselves, are not treated in many textbooks. In addition, problems and solutions often cross boundaries between what were once considered separate disciplines of study. The student or manager seeking a learning aid in an era of change will frequently be frustrated. In many respects, materials which have been available do not reflect either the new developments or the unprecedented opportunities for creative thinking and problem solving which accounting presents.

Each book in this Addison-Wesley Series treats a new development or subject which has not been widely treated in textbooks which are widely available. In addition, because each book concentrates on a single set of problems, methods, or topics in accounting, each provides comprehensive coverage in an economical form. The Series was conceived to help all who work with or process accounting information, all of whom must continue to learn in order to keep pace with the changes which are occurring. Each book has been carefully developed by an outstanding scholar.

Books in this Series were prepared in the belief that the evaluation of accounting and its importance to managers will continue, and with faith that books are an effective means to assist all who are interested to participate in the developments which will take place in the future. Our goal has been to improve the practice and processes of accounting, and to help all who use accounting information to do so more effectively.

William J. Bruns, Jr.
Professor of Business
Administration
Harvard University

PREFACE

Recent events in the field of accounting have brought the activities of accounting policy makers into the forefront. Much debate has emerged over the role of the standard setter and the process of resolving accounting controversies. These discussions have led to recognition of the pervasive nature of accounting standards. Prescriptions have emerged imploring policy setters to consider the economic consequences of their activities, or the impact of external financial reporting standards on all sectors of society.

While the evolutionary state of the standard-setting function has been the topic of conferences and discussed in accounting journals, no one treatise exists which sets forth the available evidence, examines all the arguments, and formulates the policy-making process from a broad societal perspective. As a result, accounting educators present at best a fragmented picture of the realities of the accounting environment. Students enter the business world believing controversial accounting issues are resolved with theoretical and technical solutions. They soon experience the political nature of accounting when forced to consider reporting issues from the context of vested interests. If they become corporate managers, they are interpreting external financial reporting issues in a manner consistent with their own self-interests. If they enter the accounting profession, they are subjected to the pressures of corporate clients motivated by self-interests.

By studying the policy-making process as it is developing, this book provides a means for realistically examining present-day accounting standards and considering the resolution of future issues. Identification of the various factors which impinge on the process, and integration of these factors into a policy-setting framework, facilitates an overall understanding of the role of accounting policy making in society. Because this role is still evolving, portions of the framework are likely to be controversial. Some may argue against the important role accorded management in the process, maintaining the financial statement user still reigns supreme. Pure accounting theorists may cling to the notion of reality in financial reporting. The intent of the book, however, is to develop a framework consistent with events as they have developed in the accounting environment. This purpose compels a broader conception of policy making which encompasses the business community.

The book has a variety of potential uses in upper division undergraduate, masters, and doctoral courses. The topics of the book correspond with the material covered on complex disclosure issues in the latter portions of Intermediate Accounting courses, and can be used to tie together seemingly unrelated topics. The book can be used as supplemental to a basic intermediate accounting text as follows: Chapters 1, 2, and 3 would be used initially to establish the framework for formulating accounting standards; Chapters 4 through 7 would be used in conjunction with the technical treatment of topics such as foreign currency translation, inflation accounting, oil and gas accounting, earnings per share, leases, segment reporting, and forecasts; and Chapter 8 would serve to interrelate the material.

The book can be used in a similar manner as a supplemental text in Advanced Accounting courses covering the practical aspects of specialized reporting problems, stressing the impact of accounting policy or the formulation of standards governing topics such as accounting for business combinations. Courses that use a casebook approach to resolving financial reporting issues can be structured around the framework provided in this book, giving students a foundation for considering such problems from both a corporate and policy viewpoint.

In seminars and discussion courses on disclosure and policy issues, the book can be used as the main text or one of several monographs which focus on special topics. For advanced seminars on financial reporting issues stressing research aspects, the book provides a basis for studying the articles referenced in more depth. The book can also be used in basic courses on Accounting Theory which consider the theoretical structure of accounting from a normative context. Used as supplementary to an accounting theory text, the book enables students to juxtapose the theory with a policy approach to resolving issues.

The book has further use in other specialized courses. For advanced courses in Public Accounting, the book is important for considering the role of the CPA vis-à-vis policy makers and corporate management. In Financial Statement Analysis courses, the book enhances an understanding of the impact of accounting policy on the use of information contained in external financial reports. Courses on Government and Business can use this book to consider the effect of accounting regulation on the business community.

Beyond its use in the university setting, this book is also important to corporate executives and CPAs who are confronted with making financial accounting decisions. The book can be used in continuing education programs sponsored by professional organizations and colleges; inhouse training programs; and self-study to gain an understanding of the accounting environment, how to deal with the firm's CPAs, interface with corporate clients, communicate with accounting policy makers, and approach the resolution of reporting issues.

The policy-making process developed in this book is largely within the context of a sociological approach to engineering change. This orientation has necessitated the use of concepts and terms specialized to the field of sociology. While efforts have been made to reduce the sociological jargon, the unique meaning of concepts such as planned social change, innovation, change agent, and change target made their use inevitable. Additionally, the field of accounting itself is replete with acronyms and abbreviations. An attempt has been made to use the most common symbolization, and a list of abbreviations has been provided.

Many people have contributed to the completion of this book. The financial support of the Graduate School of Management at UCLA during the summers of 1978 and 1979, allowing me to freely pursue my ideas, is gratefully acknowledged. I am appreciative to Susan Corley for typing initial portions of the manuscript, and to Nancy Donohue and Jamie Tongue for professionally typing the final drafts. The research assistance of Ken Low, Winston Cheong, and Carol Nau was invaluable. Philip Defliese provided helpful insights into some of the issues faced by the Accounting Principles Board, and Paul Brown offered some important observations on the current standard-setting process. The support and cooperation from William

Hamilton, Editor of the Business and Professional Division at Addison-Wesley and William Bruns, Jr., Consulting Editor for Addison-Wesley greatly facilitated completion of the book. Finally, I am indebted to Grant W. Newton for his encouragement early in the project, and for his patience when it later became an intrusion.

Los Angeles, California L. K. N.
April 1980

LIST OF ABBREVIATIONS

AICPA	American Institute of Certified Public Accountants
APB	Accounting Principles Board
ARB	Accounting Research Bulletin
ASR	Accounting Series Release
CAP	Committee on Accounting Procedure
CPA	Certified Public Accountant
FAC	Statement of Financial Accounting Concepts
FAS	Statement of Financial Accounting Standards
FASAC	Financial Accounting Standards Advisory Council
FASB	Financial Accounting Standards Board
FAF	Financial Accounting Foundation
FEI	Financial Executives Institute
NAA	National Association of Accountants
SAB	Staff Accounting Bulletin
SEC	Securities and Exchange Commission

A monkey and a fish were caught in a sudden flood. The monkey scrambled up a tree to safety. Noticing the fish struggling against the current, the monkey was filled with humanitarian desire and rescued the fish from the water. To the monkey's surprise, the fish was ungrateful for this technical aid.

(Adams, 1960, as quoted by Rogers, 1972, p. 194.)

CONTENTS

1 The Regulation of Accounting Disclosures 1
   Overview of the Book 4

2 The Formulation of Accounting Policy 7
   The Current Policy-Setting Mechanism 7
      FASB: Organization and Procedures 8
      SEC: Organization and Procedures 10
   Orientations to Resolving Accounting Controversies 13
      Reporting Economic Reality 14
      User Orientation 14
      Orientations of the FASB and SEC 17
      Deficiencies of Normative Approaches 20
      Supplier Orientation 23
   Summary 24

3 A Socio-Political Framework for Setting Accounting Policy 26
   A Sociological Perspective 26
      An Economic-Consequences Approach 26
      The Role of Corporate Management 29
      Planned Social Change through Accounting Policy 31
   A Framework for Engineering Change through Accounting Policy 34
      Identifying a Need for Change 35
      Acceptance of Policy Setters 36
      Consideration of Outside Views 39

Management Value Schemes in Financial Reporting..............44
　　　Assessment of Potential Consequences........................45
　　　Monitoring the Results of Policy Decisions.....................48

　　Summary..51

4　The Role of the Accounting Policy Maker........................53

　　The Power Position of Accounting Policy Setters..................53
　　　Types of Power Bases.......................................53
　　　The Coercive Power of the SEC..............................54
　　　The Legitimate Power of the FASB...........................56

　　Structural Conditions of Power.................................61

　　The Relationship Between the FASB and SEC.....................62
　　　Relative Power Positions....................................62
　　　Recent Power Struggles.....................................65

　　Summary..71

5　Strategies for Promulgating Accounting Standards..................72

　　Types of Strategies...72
　　Strategies Used in the Private Sector...........................74
　　　The APB..74
　　　The FASB...77

　　Strategies Used by the SEC....................................80

　　The Promulgation of Policy to Enhance Change..................85
　　　In the Private Sector.......................................85
　　　In the Public Sector..86

　　Summary..88

6　Factors Influencing Management's Reaction to
**　　Accounting Standards..90**

　　General Forces Resisting Change...............................90

　　Aspects Specific to the Innovation..............................91
　　　The Importance of Perceptions..............................91
　　　Relative Advantage..93
　　　Compatibility with Norms...................................98

Complexity in Use..100
Trialability of the Change..................................102
Observability of Perceived Benefits..........................104

Communication Aspects......................................105

Social System Effects in the Accounting Environment..............106

Summary...108

Appendix to Chapter 6—Previous Research on Management's Adoption of Accounting Changes..............................109

Characteristics of Accounting Standards as Innovations...........109
    Accounting Changes for Tax Benefits.........................109
    The Adoption of LIFO.......................................111
    Purchase versus Pooling of Interest...........................112
    Installment Reporting for Tax Purposes........................112
    Accounting for Inflation......................................113
    Replacement-Cost Disclosures................................114

Alternative Theories of Management's Accounting Policy Decision...115
    Income Smoothing..115
    Functional Fixation...116
    Learning Set...116
    Corporate Personality.......................................117

7 Compliance with Accounting Policy............................120

Accounting Innovation Decisions...............................120
    The Innovation Decision Process..............................120
    Types of Adoption Decisions..................................121
    The Decision to Use Authority................................124

Conformity to Accounting Policy................................128
    Behavioral Compliance......................................128
    Attitudinal Acceptance......................................130

Opposition to Accounting Standards............................133
    Criticism of the Innovation...................................133
    Challenges to the Policy Maker...............................135

Accounting Changes Over Time.................................138

Summary...140

8 A Reexamination of Accounting Policy Making................... 141
   The Importance of a Sociological Perspective..................... 141
   A Policy-Making Model.. 143
   Implications of the Model..................................... 149
      Accounting Policy Makers................................. 149
      The CPA Profession....................................... 155
      Corporate Management.................................... 156
      Accounting Theory and Research........................... 158
   Summary.. 162
   References... 163
   Index... 173

Chapter One

THE REGULATION OF ACCOUNTING DISCLOSURES

External financial reporting became a critical factor in business and commerce with the increase in separation between the owners and management of firms, and the widespread growth in public ownership of business entities. Current and potential investors increasingly depended on the firm's external report of its financial condition for knowledge about the entity's operations. Concern with the adequacy of this information, and the alleged contribution of abuses in external reporting practices to the security market failures of the 1930s, led to the regulation of the corporate disclosure system. This regulation focuses on developing prescriptions regarding financial reporting practices to be followed by corporate management in disclosing information to the public. In essence, the responsibility for determining the nature of the firm's disclosures has been moved from management to an independent regulatory body.

Justification for regulation of the accounting system relies on the existence of market imperfections which indicate that free-market forces would result in suboptimal corporate disclosures. Two types of economic arguments are cited as support for the regulation of external financial accounting (Gonedes and Dopuch 1974, pp. 65–78; Advisory Committee on Corporate Disclosure 1977, pp. 623–639; Foster 1978, pp. 539–541). The first involves efficiency, or Pareto optimality, whereby no one's well-being can be improved without harming someone else's well-being. In the absence of aberrations in the free-market system, market forces will provide an efficient allocation of resources.

Market failures can, however, thwart attainment of Pareto optimality. One type of market failure involves externalities wherein one group's actions have an effect on other parties who are not charged or compensated for these actions through the price system. Externalities arise with public goods, defined as commodities that may be consumed by nonpurchasers. External financial accounting disclosures are public goods since third parties may use the information without affecting the disclosures available for other users. Such nonpurchasers are called free riders since they benefit from the disclosures but do not pay for the information. Examples of free riders in the accounting setting include financial analysts and potential investors.

The presence of externalities means that producers of the public good have no incentive to internalize the effects on third parties. Reliance on the free-market system may lead to suboptimal production of the public good; in this case, external accounting disclosures. This gives rise to the need for some form of collective action, as through regulation. Several critical issues emerge. It is not clear that market intervention will result in efficiency. If some form of collective action is deemed desirable, which type of organization should be used becomes an important question. Ultimately, a nonmarket solution to the disclosure system involves social choice problems and complications from resolving issues in a manner consistent with individual preferences.

The second economic argument supporting the regulation of accounting disclosures involves equity issues, or the choice among efficient solutions. Even if efficient resource allocation is certain, there is no assurance from the market system that the most equitable efficiency condition will obtain. Without regulation, the inability of all investors to equally acquire information can result in undesirable resource allocation. Such arguments are used to support expansion of the disclosure system to eliminate insider information. Social choice problems are involved here also in determining the most equitable and efficient solution.

The market failures relating to the efficiency and equity of the disclosure system are used as theoretical justification for regulatory activities in the accounting environment. Agreement is not complete, however, on the need for such regulation, largely because of the lack of empirical evidence on the workings of the free-market system as compared with the regulated system. "Currently, there is little or no evidence that bears on these questions. As a result, the desirability of a mandated disclosure system is still an open issue" (Advisory Committee on Corporate Disclosure 1977, p. 652).

Despite the questionable efficacy of the regulation of external financial reporting, all indications are that such market interventions will be expanded rather than reduced. This contention is supported by the public-sector's increasing scrutiny of the private-sector's standard-setting function, and serious threats from governmental authorities to move all regulatory activities into an agency directly under the control of the federal government. Regulation of the amount and nature of corporate disclosures benefits some, but imposes restrictions or costs on others. Accounting legislation thus potentially effects resource allocation and wealth distribution in the economy. The regulation of accounting disclosures is of great interest to those whose economic welfare may be affected, and the formulation of external financial reporting requirements becomes an important social issue.

Regulation of corporate disclosures is accomplished largely through accounting policy making, defined as "the process by which individuals or groups in power choose general rules for action that may affect others within an organization or perhaps affect an entire society"(Horngren 1976, p. 90n). Technically, the regulatory function does not include activities in the private sector, since an alternative to governmental regulation is private-sector collective agreement. In the accounting environment, the great dependence of private-sector policy boards on the public sector for authority precludes separate assessment of these agencies. Interdependencies between private- and public-sector activities implies viewing both within a regulatory context.

Three parties emerge as central to the standard-setting mechanism: (1) policy makers, or those bodies with the ability to impose their will on others, (2) financial statement preparers, who must comply with accounting policies, and (3) financial statement users, who employ the outputs from compliance. Until recently, policy makers have focused on the needs of financial statement users in regulating the disclosure system. Of late, however, fuller recognition has been given to the pervasive role of accounting standards. Attention has turned to the effect of such regulation on corporate management in its role as the financial statement preparer.

A broader conception of the accounting policy-making function is facilitated by viewing the process within a socio-political framework. Two elements are critical to this framework: (1) the sociological factors that determine the characteristics of the accounting issue influencing acceptance of regulation in that area, and (2) the political forces that emerge from these sociological factors, relating to the institutional structure and the standard-setting process. The nature of the specific accounting issue addressed and the vested interests involved give rise to a politicization of the regulatory function. This broader view of the policy-making environment renders deficient complete reliance on theoretical solutions to controversial issues.

While the societal role of standard setting in accounting has become more fully recognized, little progress has been made in identifying the influencing factors and structuring them into the policy-making process. The purpose of this book is to build a framework for incorporating the sociological factors into the standard-setting function, and to relate the elements of the framework to the resolution of current issues in the accounting profession. Formalization of the policy-making process in both the private and public sectors should lead to a better understanding of the realities of the standard-setting environment. This should provide a fuller understanding of the role of policy makers, the pressures from outsiders on policy deliberations, and the means for more effective formulation of directives governing the corporate disclosure system.

OVERVIEW OF THE BOOK

The next chapter discusses current approaches to formulating accounting policies. Procedures followed in both the private and public sectors are described, and potential approaches to resolving controversial issues are considered. Chapter 3 examines the accounting function from a sociological perspective, and establishes corporate management's role in the policy-making process. A framework is then developed, incorporating six elements critical to engineering change in reporting practices through accounting policy.

The policy-making model that provides the basis for the organization of the book is depicted in Figure 1-1. The six elements central to the process of issuing an accounting standard include: (1) identification of the need for a change, (2) establishment of the policy maker's acceptance, (3) incorporation of outside viewpoints, (4) consideration of management's value schemes, (5) assessment of potential consequences from the proposed policy, and (6) attention to results from promulgated directives.

The two chapters which follow focus on the accounting standard setter within the context of the policy-making model. The role of

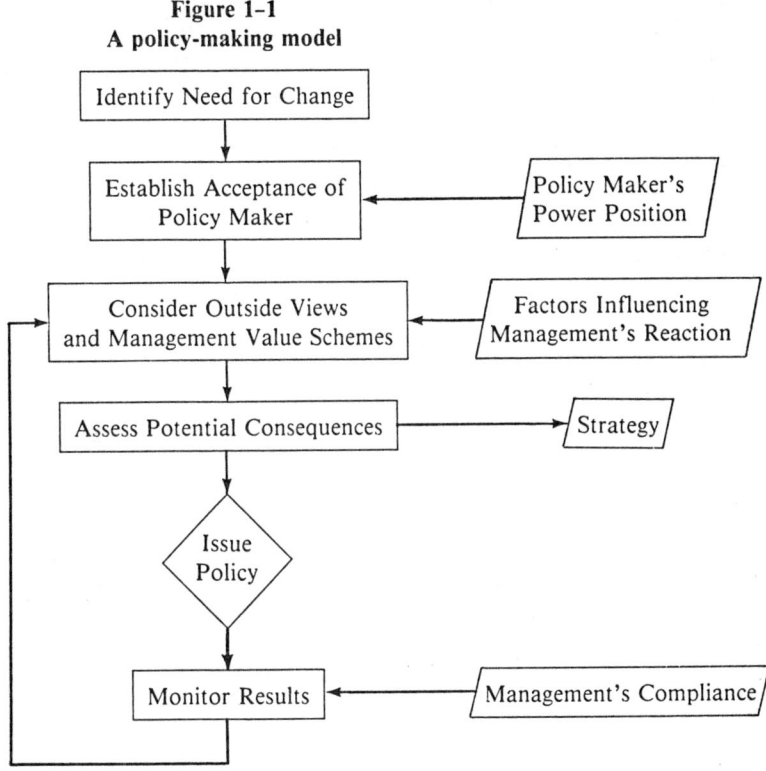

Figure 1-1
A policy-making model

policy makers is considered in Chapter 4, and their power positions are seen as important inputs to their acceptance as authoritative regulatory agents. The specific strategies used by policy makers in promulgating directives are shown in Chapter 5 as important to the effectiveness of a given standard. The choice of a strategy for enacting a particular directive results from consideration of the first five elements in the policy-making process.

Corporate management's role in formulating accounting standards is the subject of the next two chapters. In Chapter 6, the aspects of accounting standards which influence management's stance regarding a policy are identified, shown as inputs to the consideration of outside views and value schemes, and related to the effectiveness of the standard. The process by which management conforms to a directive, including behavioral and attitudinal responses, is shown in Chapter 7 as critical to monitoring the results from an accounting regulation. Also discussed are the means used by the corporate community to express opposition to accounting policies.

The socio-political framework is reexamined in Chapter 8. The elements of the policy-making model are more fully integrated with the various inputs to and outputs from the process. Implications of the model are drawn to accounting policy makers, the auditing profession, corporate management, and accounting theory and research.

Chapter Two

THE FORMULATION OF ACCOUNTING POLICY

Formal procedures for the establishment of financial reporting standards in both the private and public sectors are fairly well-established. Disagreement exists, however, over the objectives policy setters should pursue in issuing disclosure requirements. The purpose of this chapter is to examine the current structure for developing accounting practice and reporting requirements, and to consider the orientations that might be adopted by policy makers when resolving accounting issues.

THE CURRENT POLICY-SETTING MECHANISM

Various organizations have been involved in the establishment of accounting standards. Federal agencies concerned with external financial disclosures include the Securities and Exchange Commission (SEC), Federal Trade Commission, Treasury Department, and Department of Energy. State regulatory commissions are concerned with conformity to accounting standards by public accountants. In the private sector, accounting policy has been promulgated by the Committee on Accounting Procedure (CAP), Accounting Principles Board (APB), and Financial Accounting Standards Board (FASB). These latter groups have involved individuals from the public accounting profession, business community, and financial analyst sector in the resolution of accounting issues.

Two organizations currently dominate the establishment of accounting standards to be followed by corporations issuing financial reports. The FASB formulates requirements for financial statements prepared in accordance with generally accepted accounting principles and examined by Certified Public Accountants (CPAs). The SEC issues accounting practice and disclosure requirements for corporations with securities publicly traded. Both policy-setting bodies have established procedures and pronouncements for promulgating accounting standards.

FASB: Organization and procedures

By the late 1960s the APB, predecessor to the FASB for the establishment of accounting principles in the private sector, was receiving severe criticism. The APB's ineffectiveness was attributed to its inability to resolve major reporting issues, slow response to urgent problems, and neglect of viewpoints from all parties affected by accounting policy. In response to this situation, the Wheat Study Group was created in 1971 as a special committee of the American Institute of Certified Public Accountants (AICPA) and charged with studying the process of establishing accounting principles and recommending changes for increasing its effectiveness. The committee consisted of seven members: three CPAs and four representatives from the investment, academic, and business communities. The present mechanism for the formulation of accounting policy was established in 1973 as a result of the Wheat Study Group's report. Modifications were made to the structure and procedures of this mechanism following a 1977 review by the Structure Committee of the Trustees of the Financial Accounting Foundation (FAF) (Study on Establishment of Accounting Principles 1972; Financial Accounting Foundation Structure Committee 1977).

The current private-sector standard-setting system is a tripartite organization consisting of the FAF, FASB, and Financial Accounting Standards Advisory Council (FASAC). The FAF is governed by a Board of Trustees made up of eleven representatives from the six organizations sponsoring the operations of the FAF: the American Accounting Association, AICPA, Financial Analysis Federation, Financial Executives Institute (FEI), National Association of Accountants (NAA), and Securities Industry Association. Responsibilities of the FAF include appointing members of the FASB and the FASAC, obtaining funds and approving budgets for the three groups, overseeing the plans and operations of the FASB and FASAC, and periodically reviewing the mechanism for setting financial accounting standards in the private sector.

The FASB is responsible for the establishment of financial accounting and reporting standards and is authorized to conduct all activities necessary to fulfill that purpose. The only requirements for becoming one of the seven members of the FASB are knowledge of accounting, finance, and business, and a concern for the public interest. After relinquishing all affiliations held prior to being appointed to the FASB, members serve full time for up to two terms of five years each and attempt to remain independent of outside pressures and interest groups.

The FASAC has a minimum of twenty members who are chosen to provide a broad representation of the FASB's constituencies. The purpose of the FASAC is to serve in an advisory capacity to the FASB by consulting with it regarding major technical issues, its agenda of projects and priorities, the appointment of task forces, and comments regarding proposed and effective pronouncements.

The FASB issues several types of pronouncements for the establishment of financial accounting and reporting standards. Statements of Financial Accounting Standards (FAS) are used to formulate policies regarding the accounting for and presentation of financial information. Statements of Financial Accounting Concepts (FAC) are used to establish the theoretical foundations underlying financial accounting and reporting standards. Interpretations are also issued by the FASB to clarify, explain, or elaborate an FAS, FAC, Accounting Research Bulletin (ARB), or APB opinion.

Prior to issuing a policy statement, the FASB follows certain rules of procedure designed to facilitate a thorough study of the issues and broad public participation in the process (FASB 1978f). The FASB's due process involves opening all deliberations to the public, maintaining a complete public record, and encouraging communication of opinion from its constituencies. Development of operating and project plans is the responsibility of the Chairman of the FASB. The Screening Committee on Emerging Problems, comprised of representatives from the FASB, FASAC, and other interested parties, evaluates and advises regarding emerging accounting problems. All operating and project plans, including the agenda of specific projects and their priority, must be approved by the FASB.

The FASB's due process defines steps that are usually followed for major projects. Once a specific issue is approved and given a priority, the Director of Research and Technical Activities assigns one or more members of the FASB technical staff to work on the project. With the advise of the FASB, Director of Research and Technical Activities, and FASAC, a task force is appointed by the Chairman of the FASB consisting of individuals with an expertise or viewpoint relevant to the issue. The task force is important for maintaining communication between the FASB and its constituents. The functions of the task force are to advise on defining the problem and the scope of the project, assess the need for additional research, and assist in preparing a discussion memorandum. Research projects may be undertaken during this period by both the technical staff of the FASB and outside individuals on specific issues related to the project.

A discussion memorandum is often prepared, designed to be a neutral document setting forth a definition of the problem, the scope of the project, the financial accounting and reporting issues involved, relevant literature and research findings, alternative solutions under consideration, and the arguments and implications of each alternative. A summary of the discussion memorandum may also be issued, containing a description of the major issues in less technical terms, thus encouraging broader public participation in the policy-formulation process. The discussion memorandum is widely distributed with written commentary invited, often forming the basis for a public hearing. When a public hearing is held, all interested individuals are given the opportunity to make oral presentations and provide written position papers regarding their viewpoints on the issues. An exposure draft of a proposed FAS or FAC may result from this process, and it is subsequently released for public review. Written comments are received by the FASB, providing input for any modifications in the FAS or FAC. A second public hearing may be deemed necessary to consider further the comments. A statement is issued when at least a majority of the FASB members approve of the final document.

SEC: Organization and procedures

As a result of the security market failures of the 1930s, the U.S. government concluded that among the reforms needed to enhance efficient allocation of the economy's resources was fuller disclosure of information regarding securities publicly traded. The Securities Act of 1933 and the Securities Exchange Act of 1934 were accordingly passed. While both acts emphasize the disclosure of information, the former concerns the registration of securities prior to initial sale to the public and the latter concerns periodic reporting by firms whose securities are publicly traded.

The SEC was created by Congress in the Securities Exchange Act of 1934 as an independent agency to administer several regulatory laws, including the 1933 and 1934 Acts. It is primarily responsible for establishing the reporting requirements for firms filing financial statements under the latter two acts, and it has been given the authority to define the form, content, and accounting rules governing those filings. It is a five-member bipartisan committee, appointed by the President of the United States with one member designated as chairman. A professional staff has been established and organized into offices and divisions to assist the SEC in the performance of its duties. Most closely involved in accounting issues are the Division of Corporate Finance and the Office of the Chief Accountant.

The Division of Corporate Finance has broad responsibility for preventing fraud in the securities markets resulting from the issuance of false or misleading information. It thus issues disclosure standards to be met by all firms filing information under the reporting requirements and it enforces compliance with those standards. The Office of the Chief Accountant acts as the primary advisor to the SEC on all accounting and auditing issues. This responsibility involves informing the SEC about problem areas, conducting research, communicating with interested parties regarding financial reporting matters, developing accounting and auditing standards, and monitoring compliance with financial reporting regulations.

In fulfillment of its duty to formulate requirements for reporting under the 1933 and 1934 Acts, in 1940 the SEC issued Regulation S-X. The SEC also promulgates Accounting Series Releases (ASR) while its staff issues Staff Accounting Bulletins (SAB). Regulation S-X is periodically revised and sets forth the general form and content of financial statements to be filed with the SEC. ASRs are used to deal more extensively with accounting practice and disclosure regulations needing special treatment. SABs are interpretative pronouncements to disclose the staff's views on specific reporting issues and to guide registrants in implementing the SEC's regulations.

The procedures followed by the SEC in creating financial reporting regulations are purposely kept flexible and informal, enabling it to be responsive to changing conditions. Accordingly, its disclosure requirements are often formulated through indirect and ad hoc means: comments on filings with the SEC, initiation of enforcement proceedings, discussion of controversial issues in Commissioners' speeches, etc.(Golub 1979; Advisory Committee on Corporate Disclosure 1977, p. 332). The general process to be followed by the SEC in establishing policy is governed by Section 553 of the Administrative Procedure Act, which establishes the mechanism for agency rule making. The requirements include general notice of a proposed rule, solicitation of views from interested parties, statement of the basis and purpose of an adopted rule, and receipt of petitions by outside persons desiring the repeal of a rule.

The rule-making process begins with the appointment of a group of SEC staff members with responsibility for the project ("The SEC Rulemaking Process" 1978). Although it works within the framework of the Administrative Procedure Act, the SEC has not formalized procedures for considering the views of outside parties prior to issuance of a proposed rule. The primary mechanism for soliciting such views has been through public hearings at which interested persons can present their positions. Such hearings, however, are not held in all cases. Instead the process often begins with the publication of a proposed rule based primarily on the SEC's experiences and beliefs. Comment letters on the proposal are received and considered by the staff, in conjunction with the need for a ruling and the perceived public interest, to formulate its advice to the SEC for final action. This recommendation comes in the form of a document containing a statement of the issues, reasons for the suggested solution, potential consequences from its adoption, comment letters, and a draft of the proposed ASR. An open meeting is held by the SEC, any modifications deemed necessary are made, and the ASR is issued.

Concerned with the present system of corporate disclosure and its role in that system, the SEC created an Advisory Committee on Corporate Disclosure in 1975. Composed of seventeen members representing the interests of accountants, lawyers, corporate executives, and financial analysts, the Advisory Committee was charged with reexamining the disclosure system created by the 1933 and 1934 Acts. In its final report issued in November, 1977, the Advisory Committee concluded that the structure of the present disclosure system and its implementation and development by the SEC are sound and in no need of radical reform or renovation. Three recommendations were made, however, with direct implications for the procedures followed by the SEC in its policy-making activities (Advisory Committee on Corporate Disclosure 1977, pp. 332–336).

First, it was recommended that indirect means for establishing disclosure requirements should be used only on a temporary basis. Instead, the rule-making process should be initiated as soon as the SEC has isolated a reporting issue. Second, the Advisory Committee urged publication of a concept release prior to proposing a rule that involves major conceptual issues in an area where the SEC has little previous experience. While not required in all instances, such a document would be valuable for alerting the public to emerging issues, exposing the SEC's views, and soliciting the comments of interested parties. These comments would be incorporated in the proposed rule, along with the outcome of any public hearings, thus broadening outside participation in the policy formulation process. The final recommendation of the Advisory Committee was that the SEC should recognize that the rule-making process is culminated by the prompt withdrawal of concept releases and proposed rules which have not been acted upon. Such proposals should be deemed withdrawn if not adopted or modified and reproposed for comment after a specified period of time.

The SEC's response to the first two suggestions was somewhat noncommittal (SEC 1978a). It vowed to remain alert to the need for promptly initiating the rule-making process, and it stated that experimentation with issuing concept releases had begun and would be continued. It rejected the third recommendation, claiming that the formulation of deadlines for automatically terminating policy making in important areas does not seem desirable since the difficult nature of many of the issues precludes adherence to a predetermined timetable.

ORIENTATIONS TO RESOLVING ACCOUNTING CONTROVERSIES

Accounting policy makers concerned with establishing financial reporting standards must at least implicitly consider the objectives their promulgations are to pursue. Such goals define the orientation adopted when resolving accounting issues and necessitate that standard setters make value judgments. Thus the formulation of policy includes not only the adoption of a particular theory related to an issue, but also the acceptance of an objective.

On a general level, agreement appears to exist that the purpose of financial reporting is to provide economic data about business entities. Debate arises over specification of the user of accounting disclosures and the environment surrounding the preparers and users of the information. Numerous paradigms emerge, each of which offers a particular definition of a given accounting issue and approach for resolving the problem. (Committee on Concepts and Standards for External Financial Reports (1977) discusses the various paradigms in accounting theory and the implications to resolving policy issues.) Three general categories of orientations for setting accounting standards can, however, be identified: (1) reporting economic reality, (2) enhancing the usefulness of disclosures to information users, and (3) attending to the role of the information supplier.

Reporting economic reality

Resolution of reporting issues, from both a theoretical and policy vantage, has often been dominated by prescriptive or normative considerations; that is, what "good" financial reporting "should be." Emphasis is placed on correspondence between accounting measures and the economic attributes of the business entity. Concepts such as income and value are defined in an economic context (e.g., an asset is the present value of its future service potential), and alternative accounting measurement techniques are assessed by their ability to approximate these concepts (e.g., current cash equivalent, replacement cost). Noteworthy in this orientation is the assumption that an accounting system reflecting the economic reality of the firm will provide sufficient information for all potential users. Considerations relating to the decision processes of the users are thus unimportant.

Emphasizing economic reality is seen in the formulation of accounting standards where measurement issues are stressed and conceptual solutions are sought for technical issues. Prior to the 1970s, accounting policy makers predominantly considered such technical matters, focusing on the measurement of asset values and income while stressing the "fair presentation" of the firm's financial position and results of operations.

User orientation

A second approach to formulating accounting policy stresses the role of the information receiver. Focusing on the utility of accounting disclosures in making decisions, emphasis is placed on either the decision makers and behavioral ramifications from information or the decision models of the users.

The decision-maker approach to the decision-usefulness orientation emphasizes reactions to accounting data from two perspectives: (1) the individual-user viewpoint which studies the behavioral facets of accounting disclosures, and (2) the aggregate-market-level stance which focuses on the reactions of stock market prices to the disclosure of accounting data. Research in this second area has supported the proposition that the aggregate stock market is efficient, and stock prices fully reflect all publicly available information. Credence in the efficient market hypothesis has implications for accounting policy makers (Beaver 1973). (See Dyckman, Downes, and Magee (1975) for a review of the theory and research on the efficient market hypothesis.) If the aggregate market is sophisticated in using accounting information, many policy issues involving choices from alternative reporting methods are unimportant. As long as the financial statement user has adequate information for adjusting to alternative measurements, the form in which the information is presented is not significant. Substantive policy matters relate to disclosure questions or whether an item should be reported, and not measurement issues or how it is to be disclosed.

The decision-model approach to the decision-usefulness orientation emphasizes the information needs of decision makers and studies the decision processes of users. Normative characteristics of accounting information such as relevance, reliability, timeliness, and comparability are used as criteria which disclosures should fulfill to enhance the usefulness of the data to the information receiver. Emphasis on the user was explicitly admitted as central to accounting policy formulation by the AICPA's Study Group on the Objectives of Financial Statements: "The basic objective of financial statements is to provide information useful for making economic decisions" (Study Group on the Objectives of Financial Statements 1973, p. 13). In elaborating on this objective, the Study Group asserted that concern with the ability of accounting information to fulfill users' needs should take precedence over the process of measuring and reporting the data, thereby explicitly deemphasizing the concept of reporting economic reality.

This orientation is also professed by former FASB member Oscar S. Gellein (1978). He views the purpose of accounting as providing reliable and useful financial information to enhance efficient allocation of the economy's resources. Focus must therefore be on those parties making economic decisions regarding a business entity based on accounting information, primarily investors and creditors. To formulate policies that foster an efficient allocation of resources, Gellein asserts that accounting standards should strive for evenhandedness: reporting uncertainties and returns from investment in a firm in like ways for similar circumstances.

Donald J. Kirk, current Chairman of the FASB, maintains that accounting policy formulation in the private sector is, and should be, a regulatory process (Kirk 1978). This involves legislative aspects by which authoritative rules are issued, and judicial aspects by which those rules are interpreted. According to Kirk, however, the FASB should not operate in a typical legislative fashion, seeking compromise in the views of all those interested in a particular issue. Instead, accounting standards need an unswerving orientation, and, in Kirk's opinion, the focus should be on the needs of financial statement users. He accordingly asks the business community to accept the primacy of the information receiver in the resolution of accounting policy issues.

The normative criteria stressed in the decision-model user orientation have been interpreted as neutrality in policy making (Solomons 1978a, 1978b). The two principal characteristics that accounting data should possess to enhance their utility are relevance to the decision and reliability of the measurement. Relevance is of first concern in policy issues, since irrelevant data are useless regardless of their reliability. Given that the disclosures are relevant, policy choices should attempt to enhance the reliability of the data. Reliability is interpreted as representational faithfulness, or the extent to which the data depict what they purport to represent. Reliability may be closely related to neutrality, whereby the data are prepared with no intention of inducing a specific behavioral response. If financial information is representationally faithful, it must also be neutral, for if the data are presented for the purpose of effecting a particular response, they cannot be relied upon.

Stressing the criteria of neutrality, representational faithfulness, and reliability implies that accounting standards should be judged by the accuracy of the resulting information. According to this view, emphasis on fulfillment of political objectives rather than on the reliability of the disclosures may contribute to a complete loss of credibility for financial reporting. Instead, policy setters should strive for representational faithfulness. FAS No. 2, necessitating expensing of all research and development costs when incurred, may be cited as an example of the FASB's neglect of accuracy. If past research costs are expected to provide future benefits, representing the value of such expenditures as zero is not reflective of the circumstances and thus is bad "cartography."

Orientations of the FASB and SEC

The orientation adopted by accounting policy makers is heavily influenced by their sources of authority. The FASB derives a significant amount of its legitimacy from the SEC and must respond to Congressional investigations into its activities. The SEC, on the other hand, is directly dependent on Congress for its standard-setting authority. Thus ultimately both policy boards are subject to the jurisdiction of the legislative branch of the U.S. government. Since an overriding objective of Congress is to enhance social welfare, it will expect those organizations under its purview to function in the public interest. Resolution of accounting policy issues inconsistent with the public interest will encourage scrutiny and perhaps restriction of the policy boards' activities. Incentives exist in the system for both the FASB and SEC to at least appear to pursue social-welfare goals.

Illustrative of the FASB's fundamental concern with enhancing the public interest is the following statement of purpose for its pronouncements (FASB 1978d, p. ii):

> The new series of Statements of Financial Accounting Concepts is intended and expected to serve the public interest within the context of the role of financial accounting and reporting in the economy—to provide evenhanded financial and other information that, together with information from other sources, facilitates efficient functioning of capital and other markets and otherwise assists in promoting efficient allocation of scarce resources in the economy.

Elsewhere, the FASB has stated that its principal purpose is to issue pronouncements intended to improve standards of financial accounting and reporting for the guidance and education of the public (FASB 1978f, p. 1).

In narrowing this public-interest orientation, the needs of the financial statement user have dominated. This is seen most clearly in FAC No. 1, the FASB's statement on the objectives of financial reporting. The purpose of financial reporting is stated as providing information useful for making business and economic decisions regarding the use of scarce resources. The objectives of financial reporting should emanate from the needs of these users, and those needs in turn depend on the type of economic activities and decisions of concern to the users. Furthermore, the objectives should be oriented to the needs of external users because of the inability of such parties to obtain all the information they may desire from the business entity and their concomitant dependence on the disclosures made by management.

The following broad objective of financial reporting is stated by the FASB (1978d, p. 16): "Financial reporting should provide information that is useful to present and potential investors and creditors and other users in making rational investment, credit, and similar decisions." This objective is narrowed further to focus on providing information to investors and creditors for assessing future cash flows from ownership or credit investments in the firm.

This purpose of financial reporting clearly emphasizes the decision usefulness of disclosures to information receivers. Deemphasis of the economic-reality orientation, or "truth" in reporting, is seen in the FASB's assertions that accounting measures are approximations resulting from estimates, classifications, summarizations, judgments, and allocations. Thus, for example, while expensing all research and development outlays may be inconsistent with economic concepts of an asset that require the capitalization of costs with future service potential, such an approach is consistent with a user orientation aimed at portraying the risks and returns of the enterprise. Nor is the FASB primarily concerned with corporate management's self-interests in financial disclosures. According to the FASB, management's concern with the cost, adequacy, and understandability of financial reporting relates solely to its function of communicating information for use by external parties. This implies that the needs of users are to dominate management's disclosure decisions.

The user orientation is given additional emphasis in the FASB's proposed FAC No. 2 on qualitative characteristics for assessing financial accounting disclosures (FASB 1979b). This proposed statement attempts to operationalize FAC No. 1 by establishing relevance and reliability as the primary determinants of useful information. Other characteristics influencing the efficacy of disclosure practices include timeliness, understandability, verifiability, materiality, neutrality, comparability, and costs and benefits.

The SEC's public-interest orientation arises directly from the purpose for which it was created. The 1933 and 1934 Acts were passed to increase the supply of timely and reliable corporate disclosures for investor decision making. The basic philosophy underlying this legislation was that informed investors, attempting to optimize their investment decisions, would facilitate an efficient allocation of the economy's resources. Emphasis was placed on disclosure to ensure that all investors had equal access to the same information and to provide an adequate basis for intelligent investment decisions.

The role of the SEC is thus oriented by statute to the investor, as it is charged with ensuring that sufficient, reliable information is available to the public. It is responsible for establishing reporting requirements to fulfill the legislative objective of investor protection. Of utmost concern is the complete disclosure of all material information regarding securities publicly traded. To accomplish its charge, the SEC has been given the authority to require the disclosure of any information "necessary or appropriate in the public interest or for the protection of investors" (Advisory Committee on Corporate Disclosure 1977, p. 614).

The focus on sufficient information for adequate investor decision making requires a user orientation in resolving reporting issues. Because this orientation is inherent to the SEC's decisions, the Advisory Committee on Corporate Disclosure (1977, p. 307) recommended that the SEC explicitly adopt a statement of objectives to act as a guide for the rational and consistent resolution of policy issues and to provide a standard for assessing whether the SEC's activities are effective and appropriate to its purposes. The following objective was suggested:

> The Commission's function in the corporate disclosure system is to assure the public availability in an efficient and reasonable manner and on a timely basis of reliable, firm-oriented information material to informed investment and corporate suffrage decision-making. The Commission should not adopt disclosure requirements which have as their principal objective the regulation of corporate conduct.

The Advisory Committee felt the explicit statement of an objective was especially important given that the SEC is the only governmental body with the responsibility for ensuring corporate disclosure of sufficient information for investment decisions. The SEC is charged with enhancing the disclosure of information useful to reasonably knowledgeable or sophisticated investors, thus explicitly acknowledging the primacy of the decision-usefulness orientation.

The SEC did not, however, concur with the Advisory Committee on the need for a stated objective (SEC 1978a). It felt that defining the objectives of the disclosure system more precisely would unduly restrict the SEC's ability to respond to changes in the economic environment when creating disclosure requirements. Moreover, the Advisory Committee's global statement could omit considerations faced by the SEC in resolving accounting issues. Finally, the SEC was fearful that a statement of objectives could ultimately lead to litigation regarding the SEC's effectiveness in achieving its stated goals.

Deficiencies of normative approaches

Until recently, the determination of accounting standards and disclosure policies under the economic-reality and user orientations has been dominated by normative considerations: what "good" financial reporting "should be" and how the information "needs" of financial statement users can be fulfilled. The elusive truth of economic reality has been pursued, with little recognition given to the fact that various measurements of the same phenomenon communicate information regarding some aspect of the firm's operations. Accounting standards are not neutral policies to be judged in terms of their ability to depict truth. A more realistic approach to policy formulation involves consideration of the effect of choosing a particular measurement scheme on all parties involved. This stance calls for emphasizing individuals' preferences for disclosures rather than technical or aesthetic standards such as economic value, true income, relevance, and objectivity.

Normative orientations for the resolution of policy issues have been paralleled by prescriptive formulations of accounting theories. Yet no one paradigm has been accepted as appropriate for providing a framework for the standard-setting process. This lack of paradigm acceptance has caused researchers to reconsider the role of accounting theory in accounting policy formulation. Different theories and paradigms support conflicting policies, and are thus used by standard setters to form opinions on a subjective basis. The lack of paradigm acceptance restricts the guidance which accounting theory offers to the formulation of policy. The situation can be aptly summed as follows: "accounting theory is invoked more as a tactic to buttress one's preconceived notions, rather than as a genuine arbiter of contending views" (Zeff 1973, p. 177).

Efforts by standard-setting bodies to develop conceptual foundations for their policy directives may be interpreted as justifications for decisions and reactions to criticism from constituents (Watts 1977; Watts and Zimmerman 1979). Such attempts to develop theory have not been successful because only explanations based on individuals pursuing their own self-interest would be consistent with the decisions made by policy makers. Self-interest explanations would not enhance the policy makers' position in society, however, so various normative justifications are sought to support the diverse body of accounting standards.

In this setting, the development of varied accounting theories may be attributed to the forces of supply and demand for accounting prescriptions. Through regulation of financial statement disclosures, accounting policy directives may affect the economic position of the firm. The desire to enhance the wealth of shareholders and managers gives rise to the demand for theories that justify a given position on a particular issue. Because individual interests differ, diverse prescriptions arise in response to these self-interests. Parties interested in a given accounting standard argue that their position is in the "public interest" and seek normative theories as rationales or "excuses" related to social welfare. Which rationale dominates in the resolution of an issue depends on which vested interest prevails in the political process of formulating a policy.

While accounting theorists profess that normative guidelines should be used to rationally analyze the attributes of alternative policies, theories do not always precede the emergence of a policy issue. Instead, the supply of prescriptions is related to the demand for rationales to justify the diverse positions those with vested interests wish to establish. Following the emergence of a controversial issue, a variety of normative excuses will arise as theorists are enticed to enter the controversy through rewards such as funding, reputation, prestige, students, and the like. As a result, no single normative theory will consistently explain current accounting standards or predict those that will prevail in the future.

An interesting transition in this market for excuses for supporting vested interests occurred as a result of the 1933 and 1934 Acts. Prior to the 1930s, most theories relied on economic-reality arguments and prescriptions focused on the multiple uses and objectives of accounting information. Fundamental to the passage of the 1933 and 1934 Acts was the belief that full disclosure was necessary to the public interest. Market forces were alleged insufficient for ensuring adequate reporting, and thus current practice became deficient as a standard for judging disclosure policies. Policy makers needed a new justification for their directives, and public-interest arguments soon surpassed reporting economic reality as the rationale. This orientation has become refined and operationalized to providing information to investors and creditors for making economic decisions.

The focus on normative issues and the misuse of theory in the standard-setting process has seriously hampered efforts to understand the accounting environment and thus aid policy formulation. The development of a positive theory of accounting concentrates instead on the reality of the policy-making process (Jensen 1976). Largely descriptive, this perspective stresses explaining the occurrence of observed phenomena in the accounting realm, the nature of the accounting function, the actions of accountants, and the impact on the various affected parties and the economy's resources. Deemphasizing economic reality and information needs, the focus is shifted to the roles, interactions, and responses of the various groups in society affected by accounting policies.

Only after such positive questions are answered can normative issues be addressed. Determination of a "preferred" accounting method is not attempted until the parties impacted by such changes have been identified, the nature of the effects has been researched, and the reactions of all interested groups have been considered. The development of approaches to policy formulation which anticipate and consider potential consequences can only follow considerable descriptive research into why accountants, business firms, investors, governmental agencies, employees, and all other interested parties behave as they do within the accounting setting. The neglect of such important issues has been offered as an explanation for the failure of normative accounting theory to impact accounting practice beyond its use to support the positions of those with vested interests. Having been developed in a vacuum, much of theory is irrelevant to the problems in the accounting environment.

The need for an infusion of realism into the standard-setting process was identified by Dale Gerboth (1972, 1973) while an AICPA staff member. Gerboth claimed that policy makers attempt to be comprehensive by formulating goals, appealing to theory, and identifying consequences. This normative approach stresses idealistic concerns which a policy setter cannot realistically fulfill. Gerboth advocates abandoning beliefs that the purpose of accounting is truth seeking based on normative ideas of income and wealth. Since these concepts are fundamentally value judgments, primary attention should instead be given to the process of operationalizing them through policy directives and to enhancing the acceptability of the resulting rules. Analogously, attempts to identify the objectives of accounting such that technical issues can be judged by their ability to fulfill such goals are fated. These normative orientations will be unsuccessful in a political process where many parties with vested interests are involved. This environment necessitates a positive approach to policy issues where all relevant groups are considered and accounting is viewed as a utilitarian act rather than a search for ultimate truths.

Supplier orientation

Focusing on the role of the information supplier comprises the third approach to the resolution of accounting policy issues. This orientation derives its theoretical foundation from the agency theory of corporations. An agency relationship is defined as "a contract under which one or more persons (the principal(s)) engage another person (the agent) to perform some service on their behalf which involves delegating some decision making authority to the agent" (Jensen and Meckling 1976, p. 308). (Also see Watts (1977) for an extension to an agency cost theory of accounting.) Within the context of a corporation, the agents are the managers and the principals are the shareholders (stockowners and bondholders).

The agency costs of this relationship, arising from the divergence between the manager's and shareholders' interests, are of three types: (1) monitoring costs are incurred by the principal to control the agent's behavior, thus reducing the amount for which the securities will be sold; (2) bonding costs are borne by the agent to insure the principal's interests will not be harmed, thus enhancing the amount received for the securities; and (3) a residual loss is incurred by the agent arising from the discounting of the firm's securities for divergences between the principals' and agent's actions. Ultimately, management bears the effect of these costs, and there is incentive for such agents to attempt to reduce them.

As a part of their monitoring activities, the firm's principals may desire financial information. If management can produce such data at a lower cost than shareholders, managers will voluntarily agree to supply audited financial statements and thereby reduce agency costs. Because of the diverse types of bonding agreements, the accounting procedures needed to fulfill these monitoring activities will vary across firms. Thus management not only has a natural interest in voluntarily supplying financial statement information, it is also concerned with maintaining flexibility in accounting methods to provide the data needed to monitor bonding agreements.

Closely related to the stewardship concept that dominated much of accounting's development, the agency theory extends this notion by stressing the incentives within the market system for management to disclose financial information. This approach differs from the user orientation where the emphasis is on providing information for investment decision making. Instead, the supplier orientation focuses on the use of information by shareholders to control management's actions. Contrary to the agency theory of accounting, the user orientation maintains that management has few incentives to provide information, and disclosures must be externally regulated.

The supplier aspects of accounting policy issues and management's vested interests in financial reporting have only recently been explicitly considered, largely through discussion of the political process of setting accounting standards and the economic consequences of alternative policies. Agency theory provides a framework for identifying the incentives within the market system motivating management's concern with financial reporting. Policy makers are becoming sensitized to this reality and giving more consideration to the role of management in the standard-setting process.

SUMMARY

The chapter began with a description of the history, structure, procedures, and pronouncements of the FASB and SEC. Three approaches to resolving accounting controversies were described: (1) focus on reporting economic reality, (2) emphasis on the utility of information to the financial statement reader, and (3) attendance to the impact of reporting requirements on corporate management as the information supplier. While early policy issues were resolved in the private sector emphasizing the measurement of economic attributes, the FASB was seen to focus on the decision usefulness of disclosures to external information receivers. The SEC has also adopted this user orientation as it strives to regulate corporate disclosures for investor decision making to enhance the public good.

Both the economic reality and user orientations are normative approaches, and the domination of specific prescriptive theories was seen to depend on the particular stance a policy setter wished to adopt. Rather than relying on prescriptions, a positive approach to analyzing the accounting environment was suggested, in which management was accorded a role in the policy-setting process. This supplier orientation revealed that market incentives exist for management to voluntarily agree to supply sufficient and reliable financial statement information.

Chapter Three

A SOCIO-POLITICAL FRAMEWORK FOR SETTING ACCOUNTING POLICY

The pervasive nature of accounting standards indicates the importance of accounting policy to corporate management. Policy formulation and management's role can be studied within a sociological context. The purpose of this chapter is to build a framework for establishing accounting standards in which policy setting is viewed as a program for planned social change incorporating political and sociological factors.

A SOCIOLOGICAL PERSPECTIVE

Because management is vitally interested in financial reporting, the effectiveness of the policy-making process may be enhanced by a broader approach to the resolution of accounting issues in which the impact of reporting requirements on management is explicitly recognized. Various aspects of a specific standard will be important to those affected by the directive. These sociological factors become the impetus to a politicization of the standard-setting process. Scrutiny of the impact of a standard necessitates a sociological framework to incorporate and relate all the relevant social and political variables.

An economic-consequences approach

Discussion of the sociological aspects of accounting policy formulation in the accounting literature began in the early 1970s. While management had long felt sole concentration on the financial statement user was one-sided, suggestions that policy makers broaden their orientation were late in coming. One of the first to profess the need to go beyond normative standards in formulating policy was former APB member Charles Horngren (1973, p. 61):

> My hypothesis is that the setting of accounting standards is as much a product of political action as of flawless logic or empirical findings. Why? Because the setting of standards is a social decision. Standards place restrictions on behavior; therefore, they must be accepted by the affected parties. Acceptance may be forced or voluntary or some of both. In a democratic society, getting acceptance is an exceedingly complicated process that requires skillful marketing in a political arena.

The marketing of accounting standards involves obtaining acceptance by all affected parties. Horngren depicts the responsibilities of the FASB as involving both production and marketing; that is, formulating the best possible accounting standards and ensuring such standards are accepted. The marketing aspects are seen as more difficult than production or technical considerations. Horngren suggests that a standard-setting process which encourages the acceptance of regulations may necessitate considering the theories of organizations, political action, social change, and social choice.

AICPA staff member Dale Gerboth concurred with this position and asserted that policy makers will not be evaluated on the basis of their technical abilities. Instead, they will be judged on their objectivity, representativeness, and openness to competing views. "Technical competence will be presumed and must be present, but an accounting rule-making body will not succeed on its technical competence but rather on its political competence" (Gerboth 1973, p. 479; 1972, p. 48n). Policy making is viewed within a social context involving such varied disciplines as philosophy, mathematics, psychology, sociology, political science, and economics. This broader perspective may be operationalized by focusing on the social welfare impact of accounting standards (May and Sundem 1976). The political process of establishing disclosure requirements necessitates prediction and explicit consideration of the consequences of alternative policies to all parties, and individuals' preferences for those consequences. Attention is turned to the economic consequences of accounting standards, or the impact of financial accounting disclosures on all those parties involved in making decisions either with or about accounting information.

Several possible reasons exist for the insurgence of interest in the economic consequences of accounting policy (Zeff 1978). Prior to the

1970s, controversial issues were broached by both management and policy makers within the context of a "traditional accounting" model, stressing "theoretically sound" accounting measurements. Such normative approaches have wanned for several reasons: institutions have been increasingly held publicly responsible for their actions, more complicated issues involving many vested interests are being addressed by policy makers, standards have had a larger impact on firms' financial reports, the influence from related disciplines has grown, procedural reforms attempted by private-sector policy boards have appeared inadequate, Congressional investigations have been launched, the importance of the earnings figure to management in maintaining its equity markets has heightened, accounting data are being used increasingly for social control, the influence of outsiders in resolving accounting issues has risen, and management has begun admitting that its reactions to accounting policies are based on self-interest and not adherence to the traditional accounting model.

The need for a socio-political framework for assessing the impact of reporting requirements on all affected parties is expressed in the following description of the current policy-making environment (Zeff 1978, p. 56):

> The economic consequences argument represents a veritable revolution in accounting thought. Until recently, accounting policy making was either assumed to be neutral in its effects or, if not neutral, it was not held out to the public as being responsible for those effects. Today, these assumptions are being severely questioned, and the subject of social economic consequences "has become *the* central contemporary issue in accounting."

This orientation implies that in resolving policy issues, standard setters must consider not only accounting measurement and presentation aspects, but also the potential economic and social impact of a regulation.

Agreement does not exist on the appropriate type of economic consequences which should enter the policy setters' decisions. Former FASB member Oscar Gellein (1978) identifies four categories of consequences from an accounting policy: (1) adjustment in the capital markets to a more "evenhanded" reporting of risks and returns, (2) uneconomic actions by management which adversely affect the firm's cash flows, (3) detrimental impacts on the firm's cash flows from actions by competitors, customers, and creditors, and (4) societal effects related to the nation's economy. Only the first consequence is judged as an appropriate concern to policy makers. The second impact purportedly results from management's naivety about the role and purpose of financial reporting, the third consequence may be a cost the firm must incur to be publicly traded, and the fourth effect is outside the realm of financial reporting.

An alternative viewpoint maintains that irrespective of the reason, all four consequences result from policy decisions and therefore must be explicitly confronted. Financial accounting issues are broadened to include the institutional structure of policy formulation, sources of pressures impinging on the process, procedures for considering outsiders' views, roles of interested parties, approaches to reaching final resolution, reactions by affected individuals, and other important socio-political variables which establish the realities of the policy making environment.

The role of corporate management

Management emerges as important to an economic-consequences analysis because the legitimacy of a policy board's authority for mandating changes in behavior is dependent on maintaining responsiveness to those who must comply with directives. The lack of descriptive research into management's role has been cited as a deficiency in prior accounting research: "There is much discussion in the literature regarding the 'needs' of the users of accounting reports. Why is there little or no attention paid to the 'needs' of the suppliers of accounting reports? What are the supply side forces, and what impact do they have on accounting practices?" (Jensen 1976, p. 3.)

The agency theory of corporate reporting establishes management's motive for voluntary supplying financial reports, and thereby enhancing the market for the firm's securities. Changes in accounting standards may affect the firm's equity markets, as well as management's personal wealth, thus providing an incentive for management to react to policy issues. Management holds primary responsibility for reporting the firm's financial position and results of operations. This duty involves developing adequate information systems and choosing accounting policies and procedures. In addition to the stewardship function of accounting for the resources entrusted to management's use, financial reports provide an indication of managerial performance. This information influences the demand for and price of the firm's equity and therefore the stockholders' wealth. Management's compensation is also affected through direct remuneration schemes as well as stock and stock option plans. Motivated largely by self-interest, management is vitally concerned with any change in accounting standards or disclosure policies which adversely affect the report on its activities. This vested interest, however, is not necessarily inconsistent with the shareholders' welfare.

Criticism of the consequence-analysis approach has focused on the seemingly irrational reactions of management to accounting standards (Gellein 1978; Solomons 1978a). Such actions by management may negatively impact the firm's cash flows, and they are justifiable only if the negative impact is less than the adverse effects from compliance with the standard. If compliance with the standard does not affect the firm's cash flows, management's reactions appear irrational in terms of the efficient market hypothesis which maintains that the securities markets are not misled by changes in disclosures which do not represent a substantive impact on the firm.

Fixation by management on the firm's earnings figure is held responsible for irrational reactions to reporting changes that lack immediate cash flow effects. Management is accused of implicitly believing that investors are naive, subject to confusion, and unable to discern changes in reporting practices with substantive economic impact on the firm. Irrational behavioral responses are used to discredit the importance of economic consequences in establishing policy, for if such reactions are unfounded they should not impact the resolution of policy issues.

Management's reactions, however, may be influenced more by the potential for cash flow effects than by the known effects. The net income reported under a new standard may be expected to influence future tax policy, regulatory actions such as rate proceedings, or political costs as from antitrust action, as well as the firm's bookkeeping costs (Watts and Zimmerman 1978, pp. 113–114). These four factors will affect the firm's future cash flows, stock prices, and hence shareholder and management wealth. Thus management's stance on a proposed standard and its reaction to a new policy will be determined not only by the immediate impact on the firm's cash flows, or lack thereof, but also by any foreseeable effects that might result from the change in reporting practices.

Independent of the rationality of management's reactions, not all observers of the standard-setting process agree that management should be accorded a central role in policy formulation (Horngren

1972; Moonitz 1974, pp. 64–65). Adequate consideration is supposedly given to management's views through solicitation of its opinions, direct representation on policy-making boards, and indirect influence through CPAs who function as policy setters. To grant management a larger voice would be undesirable due to the conflict between its fiduciary role and performance-reporting function. This situation can be described as a dilemma in which management is responsible for the financial statements which are a report on its activities; thus management influences the standards by which it will be judged. Responsibility for financial reporting should not, however, give management free reign in selecting the reporting form. This conflict of interests purportedly can be removed if a third party assumes the function of establishing reporting requirements.

Marshall Armstrong, past chairman of the FASB, admitted the existence of political influences on accounting policy boards, asserting that such pressures arise from management's vested interest in retaining flexibility in reporting practices (Armstrong 1977). Of utmost concern to Armstrong was reducing the diversity in accounting methods. Such a goal could only be reached if business voluntarily succumbed to policy directives, even when contrary to its self-interest, for enhancement of the "public good." This attitude represents a complete repudiation of the importance of considering economic consequences.

Such extreme views place the policy setter in the position of regulating corporate disclosures with disregard for the impact of its directives on the entity's economic position. Distrust of management can result in neglecting its interest in policy formulation. While to some observers, a third party overseer for the establishment of accounting standards may be desirable to protect investors, this does not mean policy directives should be formulated on the assumption that management cannot be trusted to responsibly fulfill its reporting function. Additionally, it is not clear that managers acting in their own self-interest do not enhance the wealth of shareholders. Carried to an extreme, an assumption of distrust results in moving the responsibility for reporting on corporate activities from management to the accounting profession.

Planned social change through accounting policy

Changes in financial reporting practices are sought by policy makers to correct situations perceived as undesirable, and the formulation of accounting policy can be studied in the context of engineering social change and gaining acceptance of innovations. Critical to developing a sociological framework for studying the process of change in financial reporting is identification of the relevant social units that must change. A social group is differentiated by its objectives, motivations, attitudes, norms, statuses, education levels, and other sociological characteristics. The study of change in accounting necessitates defining the social system as, for example, all economic agents, the business community, the accounting profession, financial statement users, governmental agencies, or whatever groups are expected to be affected by a new reporting practice. The social unit whose behavior and/or attitudes are to be influenced is referred to as the change target.

Policy setting for financial reporting by corporations involves as change targets the mangement of the firms that must comply with accounting standards, since management has responsibility for establishing its reporting policies from alternative generally accepted accounting principles. To properly define the sociological context of a proposed standard and the influence of this context on the acceptance of change, there must be an assessment of the characteristics of the business community such as perceived corporate goals (maximization of shareholder wealth), professionalism (level of education), previous experience (effects of noncompliance with accounting standards), solidarity as a group (strength of the FEI), and personal objectives (enhancement of compensation). These considerations are crucial to understanding the process of change in accounting methods, since it is the information supplier which must modify behavior. Movement to "improved" accounting practices, as called for in the normative approaches which emphasize economic reality or utility to the financial statement reader, is augmented by an understanding of the movement process itself.

Accounting policy setting by third parties is a process of planned social change whereby the impetus for enacting change and the change itself are conceived outside the social unit. A change agent external to the social system attempts to modify the attitudes and/or behavior of a target group; thus the FASB and SEC act as change agents in seeking to modify the financial reporting practices of the business community. Planned social change is oftentimes undertaken to achieve social objectives of the policy board, and it may be used if management is perceived as moving too slowly in recognizing and solving a reporting problem. Many of the FASB and SEC's policy directives result from a perceived need for change in financial reporting which is not voluntarily addressed by business firms.

Disagreement may arise regarding the policy setter's proper domain. For example, the SEC Advisory Committee on Corporate Disclosure (1977) recommended that the SEC not adopt disclosure requirements that are aimed at regulating corporate conduct, as through the disclosure of executive perquisites. In response, the SEC (1978a) rejected this recommendation by stating that Congress intended corporate conduct to be affected by disclosure. Purportedly, the SEC sees as appropriate to its activities engineering social change in corporate behavior.

Three types of approaches to rectifying a financial reporting deficiency can be followed by the accounting policy setter (Kotler 1972). First, and least severe, is a helping cause whereby the victims of the social problem are assisted through a program of aid. Focusing on the problem of inflation and its distortion of conventional financial reports, a helping cause would be to disclose the impact of inflation so that financial statement users are aided in decision making. A second approach is a protest cause, wherein the institution identified as causing the social problem is disciplined or reformed. Assuming the economic structure is responsible for inflation, enacting wage and price controls exemplifies a protest cause. Finally, a revolutionary cause results in removal of the institution responsible for the problematic situation. Returning to a barter economy and eliminating the monetary system would be a revolutionary cause for solving an inflationary condition.

Accounting policy is predominantly of the helping nature, whereby improved financial reporting as an aid to investor decision making is the goal. This approach to policy formulation emanates from the user orientation adopted by the FASB and SEC. Viewing financial statement users as the "victims" of undesirable reporting practices, policy setters attempt to modify corporate disclosures and enhance investment decision making. Policies that attempt to eliminate diversity in financial reporting and foster comparability of financial statements by mandating uniform accounting treatments are examples of helping causes. On the other hand, establishing reporting requirements such as the disclosure of questionable or illegal payments by multinational corporations may inhibit these activities, thus representing a protest cause.

Within the theory of planned social change, the new behavior or attitude that a change agent wishes to inculcate is often called an innovation. While an invention occurs with the development of a new idea, an innovation does not result until an individual becomes aware of the idea and perceives it as new. Rather than measuring novelty in terms of the time since the idea was first conceived, innovation theory focuses on subjective newness or the time when a social unit becomes aware of the idea, formulates an attitude, and reaches a decision regarding adoption (Rogers and Shoemaker 1971, p. 19). For example, the notion of reporting current values in financial statements has been discussed among accountants since the early 1900s, and thus would not be considered an invention of the 1970s. But mandating the incorporation of replacement costs in a firm's financial reports makes the idea an innovation to many managers.

Innovation theory should be applied with discretion to the process of change in accounting. Given that management is responsible for the content of financial reports, its decisions on adopting reporting practices and its reactions to mandated policies are important for understanding the process of change in accounting. A distinction should be made between management's discretionary changes or the choice between alternative generally accepted accounting principles, and nondiscretionary changes or the required implementation of an FASB or SEC policy. A strict interpretation of the definition of an innovation would support viewing all accounting changes as innovations since they represent the adoption of a practice that is new to management. The nondiscretionary changes, however, are of utmost importance in the study of change in financial reporting through accounting policy. Nondiscretionary is used broadly to include situations in which management can elect to deviate from an FASB standard or SEC directive and suffer the attendant consequences. Even where an innovation adoption decision per se is not present, management's reactions to a coerced innovation are crucial to the policy formulation process.

A FRAMEWORK FOR ENGINEERING CHANGE THROUGH ACCOUNTING POLICY

In attempting to modify the financial reporting practices of the business community, policy makers must deal with the sociological process of enacting change in a social system. Only recently has the means by which accounting innovations are introduced into the business community been considered important to gaining acceptance of policy directives. Agreement on the nature of the standard-setting process was considered critical by the FAF Structure Committee (1977, pp.

7-8, 18-20). In its report, the Committee stated the FASB has a responsibility for both the promulgation and assimilation of new standards. To facilitate this acceptance, involvement of the FASB's constituents in the total standard-setting process was stressed. Such involvement was seen as important to maintaining the viability of policy formulation in the private sector. This aspect of rule making was also discussed by the SEC Advisory Committee on Corporate Disclosure (1977, p. 329) in its recommendations: ". . . in the Committee's judgment the process by which disclosure requirements are adopted can be as important to the operation and public acceptance of the Commission's disclosure program as the objectives pursued or the substantive requirements enacted."

Explicit delineation of the policy-making process should enhance the acceptability of regulations. The framework can be built within the context of a program for planned social change containing six important elements: (1) a specific area of the corporate disclosure system is identified as in need of modification, (2) policy setters are accepted as legitimate agents for establishing financial reporting requirements, (3) communication channels are devised which allow for feedback regarding management's views on disclosure rules, (4) attention is given to the business community's norms and experiences in financial reporting, (5) ex ante assessment is made of the potential economic impact of a directive, and (6) ex post analysis of the economic consequences from adopting a disclosure requirement is conducted. These elements are highly interrelated; for example, acceptance of a standard-setting agency will be influenced by its sensitivity to outside views. Specification of the important components in the process, however, provides a framework for examining the effectiveness of current policy-formulation programs.

Identifying a need for change

The standard-setting process is initiated with the perception of a need for change in financial reporting practices. The impetus may come from several possible sources: Congress attempting to accomplish policy goals, taxing authorities advocating conformity between financial and tax accounting practices, consumer groups clamoring for social responsibility information, security analysts pressing for expanded disclosures, creditors desiring liquidity information, corporate management wishing to enhance its earnings record, or any other group having a potential interest in external financial reporting. Irrespective of the initial source of pressure for change, it is the policy maker's advocation of an innovation that begins the program for planned social change.

Of primary importance is the policy setter's ability to instill the need for change in the business community. The importance of this first step for gaining acceptance of policy directives was identified by former FEI President Charles Hornbostel (1972). In considering how management could help make the FASB successful, Hornbostel suggested that the business community take the initiative in identifying problem areas and suggesting possible changes in financial reporting practices, rather than waiting for policy makers to decide when a change is needed.

Recognition of a problem is not, however, equivalent to acceptance of the proposed solution. For example, management has agreed that some modification in traditional historical-cost financial statements is desirable during inflationary periods. But corporate resistance to the SEC's mandate for disclosing replacement costs is de facto rejection of this innovation as a solution to the problem.

Acceptance of policy setters

A second important element in a program of planned social change is approval of the FASB and SEC in their roles as change agents by the business community in its role as the change target. This acceptance is more crucial for the FASB than the SEC, since the latter group possesses Congressional authority to mandate the implementation of accounting innovations. The FASB, however, depends largely on a more tenuous position of legitimacy for gaining acceptance and support from management for proposed changes.

Being received as effective change agents requires awareness by standard setters of the sociological and political ramifications of their actions. The neglect of this sensitivity by policy makers was identified by Hornbostel (1972) who, in discussing the demise of the APB, noted several factors that can contribute to a loss of respect for a policy board: lack of business community representation leading to neglect of implementation problems from proposed changes, failure to provide for sufficient communication so that the business community could identify needed changes and understand proposed standards, insufficient research into the consequences from alternative changes, and overreaction to outside pressures from groups such as security analysts and auditors.

A broad perspective to the formulation of accounting policy has been identified as lacking in the FASB's attempt to develop a conceptual framework for the logical derivation of reporting standards (Rappaport 1977, pp. 92, 94). Focusing solely on a theoretical framework for resolving controversial issues could rouse accusations by outside parties that the FASB has neglected their interests. Rejection of the FASB, and possibly any private-sector body, as an effective change agent could follow if appeals are made to the SEC and Congress. Recognizing that changes in accounting standards involve resource and wealth redistributions, acceptance of the standard setter's role is critically dependent upon confidence in the policy-making process.

Serious challenges have recently been made to the FASB and SEC's position in society as agents for engineering change in the financial reporting practices of the business community. An investigation into the effectiveness of nine federal agencies, including the SEC, was conducted by the House Subcommittee on Oversight and Investigation, chaired by Representative John E. Moss. The Committee's report, issued in 1976, was based on limited interviews with no input from the accounting profession. Discrediting the FASB's legitimacy as a change agent, the report disapproved of the SEC's delegation to the private sector of its accounting rule-making authority and recommended that uniform accounting principles be prescribed by the SEC.

Public hearings were held on this report, during which the SEC and accountants testified that the accounting profession should be given a chance to regulate itself. Citing dissatisfaction with the AICPA's program for self-regulation and the SEC's patience with accountants, in April, 1978, Moss stated that he intended to introduce legislation to regulate the accounting profession. Such legislation was proposed in June but had not been acted upon by the end of 1978 when Congress adjourned and Moss retired.

In 1975, the Senate Subcommittee on Reports, Accounting and Management initiated an investigation of the federal government's role in establishing accounting practices, under the chairmanship of the late Senator Lee Metcalf. The impetus cited for this study was a general concern with management wrongdoings, corporate failures, and financial difficulties which purportedly arose from misleading accounting practices (U.S. Senate Subcommittee on Reports, Accounting and Management 1976). Metcalf's Subcommittee staff concluded that serious deficiencies exist in the accounting establishment and that the federal government, through the SEC, has facilitated the use of accounting practices damaging to public welfare. To the Subcommittee staff, this situation justified action by the federal government that would lead to reforms and restore public confidence in the accuracy and reliability of corporate disclosures. Among the specific recommendations of the staff report were that Congress should exercise its authority for ensuring proper accounting practices and that the federal government should directly establish financial accounting standards. The SEC's ability to perform this function was seriously questioned because of its long association with the accounting profession and its steadfast reliance on the private sector for formulation of accounting standards.

Eight days of public hearings followed the issuance of this report. As a result of these meetings, the Subcommittee modified the recommendations, stressing self-initiated reforms by the private sector in cooperation with the SEC (U.S. Senate Subcommittee on Reports, Accounting and Management 1977). The conclusions reached by the FAF Structure Committee and subsequent action for improvements by the FAF were endorsed by the Subcommittee. Areas still in need of reform were noted, however, with emphasis placed on the standard setter's inability to foster uniformity in accounting methods. The SEC was instructed to more actively oversee policy formulation in the private sector, rather than automatically accept the resulting standards, and to act more quickly when the FASB appears unresponsive to a disclosure problem.

The Subcommittee on Governmental Efficiency and the District of Columbia, under the chairmanship of Senator Thomas F. Eagleton, has taken over these inquiries into the accounting profession. Two days of hearings were held in August, 1979, at which the SEC endorsed retention of the standard-setting function by the private sector. FASB Chairman Donald J. Kirk testified that the FASB's progress in incorporating its constituents into the policy-formulation process has fostered confidence in its directives and the means by which they are promulgated (FASB 1979c). Broadening of the FASB's due process is seen as lessening resistence to its policies and encouraging "enlightened followership" by it constituents.

The present standard-setting mechanism in both the public and private sectors has barely survived two serious challenges from the federal government. On the positive side, some needed improvements in the organization and processes of policy boards did materialize. However, erosion in the credibility and acceptability of the FASB and SEC also resulted. Interestingly, these investigations were not directly initiated by the policy makers' constituencies, comprised primarily of financial statement users and preparers. The Moss probe was part of a larger study into the operations of federal regulatory agencies. Metcalf began inquiries based on his own allegations of accounting abuses. While the impetus for these investigations does not represent direct rejection of the FASB and SEC by the business community, it does establish a precedent and a mechanism for such attacks by interested parties.

Consideration of outside views

The channels through which a proposed change is communicated are a critical element in (1) the diffusion process whereby the business community first learns of an innovation, and (2) the adoption process whereby management decides whether to accept the idea and modify reporting practices. The communication mechanism must allow for feedback from those parties affected by and interested in the change. Informal as well as formal communication lines will be operant, and all avenues of input must be seen by management as having the potential for impact on the standard setter's deliberations. Pseudo solicitation of views will soon be detected and resented by the business community. Attention to outsiders' views early in the policy formulation process may help forestall embarassing situations which subsequently arise, as when fervent opposition to a regulation forces the policy board to modify its stance.

Policy makers in the private sector were quick to recognize the need for communication with outside parties (Zeff 1972, pp. 143-148, 206-209, 229; 1978, pp. 60-61). The communication lines of the Committee on Accounting Procedure (CAP), predecessor to the APB, were output oriented, with reliance placed on the dissemination of exposure drafts and subcommittee reports. The APB faced a somewhat different environment, as the standard-setting process entered the political arena in the 1960s. Increased public criticism and industry and government pressures stimulated the APB to seek input from outsiders. A dual education process resulted: the APB gained from the business community's views and experiences, and interested parties better understood proposed changes, thus enhancing support for the APB's pronouncements. Third parties were given membership on important committees, symposia with interested groups were held prior to the issuance of exposure drafts, public hearings allowing for broader participation were initiated, and exposure drafts were widely circulated. In response to these overtures, the FEI Corporate Reporting Committee created subcommittees to study the issues taken up by APB, to intensify research efforts and increase funding of private projects, and to be more vocal regarding its views both as individual members and as a group.

It soon became evident that while the APB had established the procedures for inculcating outside interests, substantive impact of such views was lacking. The apparent disregard for third parties' opinions, and the political pressure which resulted, contributed to the downfall of the APB. This shortcoming was given full recognition in developing the structure and procedures comprising the initial organization of the FASB. Broad representation was provided for in all parts of the tripartite organization. Outsiders were given ample opportunity to present their positions through membership on task forces, responses to discussion memoranda, presentations at public hearings, and comments on exposure drafts. While these communication channels were formalized and found effective in eliciting opinions from interested parties, the extent of the impact of such views on final standards remains unclear.

Changes were made in the structure and operations of the private-sector policy board as a result of the report issued by the FAF Structure Committee (1977). (Also see FASB 1978a.) As discussed below, many of the Structure Committee's recommendations were intended to broaden outside participation in the formulation of accounting policy and thus enhance public confidence in the FASB's activities.

Rather than being selected by the Board of Directors of the AICPA, ten of the eleven Trustees of the FAF are now appointed by a board composed of one member from each of the six organizations sponsoring the FAF. Additionally, the requirement that four of the seven FASB members have extensive experience in public accounting practice has been eliminated. Instead, a candidate for membership need only have knowledge of accounting, finance, and business. Pronouncements of the FASB are now approved upon concurrence of a simple majority, rather than the previously required five affirmative votes. These changes greatly increase the potential for individuals outside the public accounting profession to have a real impact on the promulgation of standards. With the initial five-vote requirement and only three nonCPA members on the FASB, it was not possible for outsiders' views to dominate policy decisions, although they could prohibit the passage of a standard. As a result of the changes, passage of a financial reporting requirement might occur over the objections of the FASB members purportedly representing CPAs' views, which oftentimes conflict themselves.

Formal procedures for the FASAC to provide input to the FASB during the initial stages of its projects have been expanded, thus enlarging the FASAC's role. Participation on the FASAC has been broadened with the increase in size to thirty-seven members. Emphasis was placed on obtaining new members with experience regarding the particular needs of small businesses, their public accountants, and financial statement users, as one step in a program for fuller consideration of their unique problems. Increased concern with the policy maker's social role was evidenced by acquiring members for the FASAC representing the public interest and by appointing a Government Relations Manager to coordinate FASB activities with federal agencies and congressional committees.

To further ensure a broader base of support, limits were set on the monetary amount any one individual or organization can contribute to the FAF. The number of contributors has been increased, as well as the total amount given from all constituents. Greater emphasis has been placed on research projects relevant to issues under FASB deliberation which are conducted outside the FASB's research program. Funding for external projects has been increased and conferences have been sponsored at which relevant findings can be presented. To the extent such research actually enters into the policy-making process, an additional avenue for outside viewpoints has been established.

Also intended to enhance communication, the sunshine principle was adopted such that all meetings of the FAF, FASB, FASAC, task forces, and other groups and committees are now open to public observation. The FASB's long- and short-range plans for technical projects are prepared on a regular basis, reviewed by the FASAC and FAF, and periodically published. Both of these changes should lessen the aura of secrecy which at times surrounded the policy board's activities. The format of the FASB's public hearings is being modified to encourage more participation and better understanding of the issues. Broader public awareness of all aspects of topics under FASB deliberation was the purpose for creating a public reference room containing all documents related to a given issue, publishing nontechnical summaries of the issues contained in discussion memoranda, publicizing technical correspondence between the FASB and interested parties on existing or proposed topics, and expanding the public speaking program.

Two modifications have been made in the documents issued by the FASB to encourage input from outside groups. First, drafts of FASB Interpretations are circulated for public comment rather than being restricted to the FASAC. Second, the FASB (1978c) has initiated a new series called Invitation to Comment. This document is intended to solicit comments on new agenda topics before, rather than after, the FASB begins its deliberations. The benefits expected from this new approach include facilitating timely action on potential problems, increasing input from interested parties prior to more serious consideration, and enabling the FASB to retain control over subsequent deliberations while utilizing the knowledge and experience of experts from its constituency. A channel is now available for outside views to influence the statement of a problem and alternative solutions contained in discussion memoranda.

The private-sector policy board has clearly recognized the importance of two-way communication with its constituency, including corporate management, for enhancing the acceptability of its promulgations. Recognizing that it is vulnerable to criticism in this area, serious attempts have been made to encourage and broaden outside participation. Equally as critical, however, is the actual implementation of these processes such that outside views are seen as impacting final policies.

The SEC's communication channels are considerably less structured. Much of the SEC's policy emerges from informal rulings related to a particular filing. The SEC staff's decision becomes precedent for similar issues, yet only input from the registrant initially involved has been received. Not only is the public unaware of the ruling, its views on the subject are neither solicited nor considered. Additionally, procedures for formal decisions culminating in ASRs are flexible. Public hearings on a particular issue are held at the SEC's discretion, during which outside views can be presented. More commonly, however, interested parties become aware of and respond to impending rules through the publication of a proposal. Comment letters are then received by the SEC. Again, however, the question of real influence becomes relevant. As an example, the SEC acknowledged receiving more than 350 letters of comment regarding Securities Act Release No. 5608 issued August 21, 1975, in which footnote disclosure of certain replacement cost data was proposed (SEC 1976). However, the SEC only stated that these comments were given careful consideration and the proposal was adopted essentially as put forth.

Changes have been made in the SEC's policy-formulation process as a result of the report issued by the SEC Advisory Committee on Corporate Disclosure (1977, pp. 330–335). If, as recommended, the use of informal and ad hoc approaches is reduced, there will be fewer disclosure requirements created in which interested parties have little opportunity to communicate their views. The Advisory Committee noted that only through the formal rule-making process will the effects on all parties be evenhanded, allowing for broad input to the deliberations rather than being restricted to the positions of individual registrants.

Modifications in the procedures followed prior to the issuance of a regulation were also suggested to increase public awareness of disclosure standards under consideration and to enhance early input of outside views into the policy-formulation process. The Advisory Committee expected improved communication channels to augment the flexibility and quality of regulation and to increase the public's understanding of SEC requirements. The major recommendation made by the Advisory Committee to accomplish these goals was the issuance of a concept release prior to the proposal for a rule. This would encourage responses from interested parties on major issues rather than on technical aspects of a rule which appears to be a fait accompli. Comments received to a concept release are to be explicitly addressed in the proposed regulation, thus lessening the appearance of capricious decisions by the SEC and enhancing the public's perception of real influence on resulting policies. One major limitation to this recommendation, however, is the Advisory Committee's suggestion that concept releases be issued only when the SEC is entering an area involving major conceptual issues in which it is inexperienced. The SEC has full discretion over when such input is to be solicited. Nor are public hearings required prior to the issuance of a proposed rule. Thus the potential still exists for the SEC to shortcircuit the communication lines with its constituencies and act in an arbitrary manner.

Management value schemes in financial reporting

To enhance the effectiveness of a program for planned social change, a policy maker must adequately consider the business community's norms, including management's perspective of the problem, as well as its needs and customs in external reporting. This element derives importance from the finding that professionals are more innovative than nonprofessionals when dealing with changes which are compatible with their values, but less innovative with respect to incompatible changes (Rothman 1974, p. 439).

A critical issue to the business community is maintaining flexibility in its choice of reporting practices. This freedom is needed by management for effective fulfillment of the monitoring activities and bonding agreements that arise from the firm's agency relationships. Flexibility is desired by management for freedom to choose those accounting procedures that enhance its performance report. Additionally, because of the complex and varied business practices of companies even within one industry, uniform accounting standards cannot make dissimilar firms comparable (Murphy 1979). Of minimum importance to management, then, is uniformity of procedures, either among firms for interfirm comparability or over time for intrafirm comparability. Concern with lowering reporting costs prompts management's preference for those rules and regulations which are operationally less complicated.

Cognizant of the responsibilities under the 1933 and 1934 Acts for financial disclosures that will not mislead investors, many companies prefer conservative reporting procedures and thus avoid practices that create wide fluctuations in reported earnings. Analogously, concern with legal liability for the adequacy of its disclosures induces management to stress objectivity rather than the use of judgment and assumptions in compiling financial data. While many of these norms may not be considered optimal from an external financial statement user's standpoint, they must be acknowledged as existing and explicitly dealt with if management's acceptance of change is to be enhanced.

The SEC has been faced with management's penchant for objective disclosures in the attempt to encourage voluntary reporting of corporate forecasts ("Enticing Companies Out on the Forecasting Limb" 1979). A safe-harbor rule was suggested by the SEC to protect companies from legal liability under the 1933 and 1934 Acts if projections prove inaccurate. As originally proposed, the burden of proof would be on the corporation to demonstrate that its forecast was reasonably based and was disclosed in good faith. The safe-harbor rule for "soft" disclosures suggested by the SEC Advisory Committee on Corporate Disclosure, and greatly preferred by the business community, required that the investor show management's projection was intentionally misleading. Significantly, in the final rule adopted by the SEC it demonstrated heightened sensitivity to the business community's needs. Modifying its original stance, the SEC required instead the party claiming injury to prove the basis for the projection was unreasonable.

Programs of planned change for encouraging modifications in reporting practices invoke different norms and customs, depending on the nature of the change. Once the policy setter has assessed the business community's value schemes and previous experiences, three courses of action are available: (1) inculcate only those changes that do not challenge existing values, (2) attempt to alter the norms of management such that the innovation becomes acceptable, or (3) manipulate the perception of the change such that it appears to be at least somewhat in agreement with existing values. The appropriateness of each approach depends on the solidarity of the norms, astuteness of the business community, and characteristics of the innovation.

Assessment of potential consequences

A fifth critical element in a program of planned change is an a priori analysis of potential results from adoption of a change. Change agents are often derelict in considering the consequences of introducing an innovation prior to encouraging its acceptance. They assume a change is needed, diffusion of the innovation is desirable, and its adoption represents success. Accounting standard setters should predict the short- and long-run effects of a policy on the business community and assess its overall desirability. Financial reporting standards can affect the resource allocation and wealth distribution patterns of an economy. Economic impact analysis focuses on the latent political and social consequences of a change in reporting practices (Buckley

1976; Rappaport 1977; Wyatt 1977). Because it is conducted prior to the resolution of a policy issue, the analysis is ex ante. Operationally, the focus is on the costs and benefits to various interest groups of adopting a given policy.

One important potential effect of an accounting standard occurs through information inductance, or the impact of a reporting requirement on management behavior (Prakash and Rappaport 1977; Rappaport 1977). Changes in accounting standards which affect the information to be disclosed by management lead it to anticipate the way those disclosures will be used by information receivers. In an attempt to avoid undesirable consequences from the disclosures, management may change resource allocation decisions within the firm, with ramifications at the industry and economy levels. Economic impact analysis includes an a priori assessment of behavioral and thus resource changes resulting from information-inductance reactions.

Greater emphasis on the need to consider the potential results from accounting innovations has accompanied criticisms of policy makers who focus exclusively on the technical aspects of standards in a vain pursuit of truth. Such standard setters allegedly have no understanding of the impact of their decisions on the allocation of resources within the economy. Supporters of truth-seeking through accounting policy counter that an economic-reality orientation leads to a value-free resolution of controversial issues. Whether ignored or not, however, economic consequences will accompany policy decisions. Acknowledging the existence of such effects enables policy makers to anticipate opposition and thus avoid unexpected reactions to suggested changes, devise programs to enhance acceptance, develop counterarguments to assuage critics, and reduce public controversy over the resolution of specific issues.

Sensitivity to economic-impact issues prior to the promulgation of a policy requires standard setters who possess a broader orientation and have qualifications beyond expertise in technical matters. Explicit formulation of the economic and social objectives which constitute the purpose for a standard also becomes necessary. A preliminary assessment of a specific issue should include the relationship of the policy to such objectives through analysis of the potential consequences and identification of the groups most likely to be affected. Communication with the business community on pending standards should incorporate economic impact analyses of all alternative solutions. Feedback from interested parties should be sought and given significant weight in evaluating the likelihood of such impacts and their desirability. Final policy statements could then include a statement of the costs and benefits anticipated from the chosen alternative, forming the rationale for the policy maker's recommendation. (See Buckley (1976, p. 15) and Rappaport (1977, pp. 96-97) for examples of how ex ante economic impact analyses might have been conducted by the FASB.)

The desirability of preliminarily evaluating potential results from policy decisions was recognized by the FAF Structure Committee (1977). While recommending that the FASB explicitly consider the costs and benefits of alternative solutions and include economic impact analyses in important exposure drafts, the Structure Committee deemphasized the importance of these considerations by stating that the FASB need not be "unduly influenced" by such potential effects. The SEC Advisory Committee on Corporate Disclosure (1977, p. 330) gave limited endorsement to the idea of economic impact analysis, stressing the need to consider potential costs of policy directives. No specific recommendations were made for modification of the SEC's policy-making process to include ex ante assessment of potential consequences.

Disadvantages do attend the analysis of economic impact by policy makers. The need for more extensive research and closer attention to resolving potential controversies may further delay the final resolution of a given issue. There exists the potential for greater confusion over the conclusions reached in formulating a policy, since standard setters will be reluctant to cite political reasons for their decisions.

Disagreement over potential consequences may arise because such analyses rely on projections of future behavior and reactions. Even if agreement exists on expected impact, normative issues regarding the desirability of latent wealth and resource effects may lead to conflict. The social-welfare implications of accounting standards might support contentions that policy should be set by government officials representing the public interest, rather than by private-sector organizations. The path is then opened for parties whose interests are hurt by a particular standard to appeal to government representatives for redress. Finally, the sheer intractability of the problem contributes to a discrediting of the importance of the analysis. While the costs of a proposed policy may be estimable, evidence on expected benefits is much more difficult to obtain.

Monitoring the results of policy decisions

Communication during the resolution of policy issues must be a two-way process: not only must the policy setter appropriately consider the views of the business community and adequately communicate reporting requirements to those affected, but feedback must also result whereby management expresses its reactions and experiences regarding the change. Such communication can be enhanced if, following the enactment of a directive, a mechanism exists for interested parties to appeal the decision. Additionally, as implementation of an innovation proceeds, policy setters should carefully follow the results while remaining open to modifications and the possibility of repealing the requirements. Ex post analysis of the consequences from an accounting standard involves monitoring responses to reporting changes from information users and suppliers, as well as the impact on the economy's resource and wealth distributions. These concerns necessitate empirical studies to determine if the effects projected from the ex ante economic impact analysis have materialized and to identify any unexpected economic consequences from a standard.

Examples of the mechanics of this approach can be demonstrated from recent FASB promulgations. Allegations were made that expensing all research and development costs when incurred pursuant to FAS No. 2 would discourage such activities by firms not wishing to depress earnings, and thus act as a deterrent to technological progress. These expectations should be examined in light of the trend in such expenditures since the passage of FAS No. 2. Restrictions contained in FAS No. 5, prohibiting the accrual of estimated losses from loss contingencies by charges against income, were alleged to encourage greater expenditures for insurance contracts for risks which previously would have been self-insured. Ex post consequence analysis would focus on changes in risk management practices.

Translation of foreign currency transactions under FAS No. 8, necessitating recognition of foreign exchange gains and losses on a net monetary position in quarterly financial statements, provided a major stimulus to the movement for policy makers to consider economic consequences. Requiring current recognition of all foreign exchange gains and losses, whether realized or unrealized, resulted in a "yo-yo" effect on reported earnings. To elude this volatility, many companies have chosen to avoid a net monetary position, hedge their exposure, or even abandon investment projects that were otherwise desirable

(Peat, Marwick, Mitchell & Co. 1977; Evans, Folks, and Jilling 1978). These real shifts in capital investments and equity financing cannot be ignored when assessing the consequences of the FASB's policy.

Several changes have been made in the FASB's procedures to more explicitly consider the ex post consequences from a standard, largely as a result of the recommendations made by the FAF Structure Committee. Task forces are no longer disbanded upon the completion of a discussion memorandum, but are consulted throughout the policy-making process and during the resolution of implementation problems that may arise. Interpretations or amendments relating to the standard are also reviewed by the task force.

Research into the impact of standards currently in force is receiving greater emphasis. A public conference was held by the FASB in March, 1978, on the economic consequences of financial accounting standards at which invited papers were presented dealing with such issues. Four outside research projects were commissioned by the FASB to study the effect on management decisions of FAS Nos. 5 and 8, and the impact on stock market prices of FAS No. 8. A postenactment review procedure has been instituted in which the FASB began reviewing standards in effect for at least two years, largely by requesting comments from interested parties on their experiences in applying such directives and using the resulting disclosures. The FASB's rules of procedures have been modified to include provisions for individuals to request that the FASB consider reviewing or reexamining a specific standard.

Results from these review procedures are beginning to materialize (Goshay 1978; Evans, Folks, and Jilling 1978; Dukes 1978). One of the projects regarding FAS No. 5 sponsored by the FASB found no impact on corporations' risk and insurance management decisions. The finding of changes in investment plans because of FAS No. 8 was previously mentioned. A second study regarding FAS No. 8 has found no impact on firms' stock prices from the increased fluctuations in reported earnings. In conjunction with the reexamination of this standard, the FASB held a meeting with major business and accounting persons involved with its implementation to discuss possible modifications.

While the increased emphasis on research into economic consequences is salutary, just as important is the belief by the business community that the findings will affect the FASB's policy decisions. Confidence in the impact of its feedback might encourage management to soften its opposition to controversial proposals. In announcing the postenactment review program, the FASB stressed that the new procedure did not commit it to actually modify existing standards. Yet the potential for impact on accounting policy appears real. As a result of the comments received on FAS No. 8, the FASB added a project to its agenda to reconsider the standard. A limited-scope amendment is being contemplated to alleviate the immediate problems from implementing FAS No. 8, while the FASB continues with its deliberations to completely revise the original reporting requirements.

The SEC Advisory Committee on Corporate Disclosure (1977, pp. 331, 336–340) noted that the SEC has not actively engaged in assessing the impact of its disclosure requirements. Its public-interest orientation implies that the SEC has a responsibility for reporting on the consequences of financial reporting standards, thus enabling the SEC and other interested parties to evaluate the effectiveness of its activities and the impact of its policies. The Advisory Committee stated that it is not the SEC's purpose to be concerned with resource and wealth distribution shifts resulting from accounting standards. But this information should be available to public representatives (e.g., Congress) for assessing the efficacy of the corporate disclosure system. Other benefits expected from explicit consequence analyses include more frequent reevaluation of current regulations and consequent elimination of unnecessary, ineffective, or obsolete rules; reduction of irrelevant disclosures which muddy corporate reports; and greater enforcement of requirements which are being evaded.

The Advisory Committee accordingly recommended that when disclosure rules involving major new requirements are adopted, the SEC should state whether it intends to monitor the realization of expected benefits and potential adverse consequences, and describe the procedures it plans to follow. The Advisory Committee did note that such monitoring programs would be difficult to institute. Its suggestions for implementing the recommendation include reissuing a directive for comment, holding public hearings on experiences with a rule, meeting with affected parties, and empirically studying stock market reactions to disclosure requirements. In connection with these monitoring activities, the SEC was asked to heighten its awareness of research conducted in academia and elsewhere and to encourage such outside research.

These recommendations for economic analyses culminated in the Advisory Committee's suggestion that the SEC include in its annual report to Congress the results of its monitoring programs in comparison with its objectives for adopting disclosure requirements. For current regulations this would include stipulating why the rule was established, how it was monitored, and the consequences that were identified. For new disclosure requirements the report would describe expected consequences and plans for monitoring its impact.

In responding to these suggestions, the SEC (1978a) concurred with the desirability for ex post consequence analyses concentrating on the effectiveness of and need for its regulations. It agreed to increase its monitoring activities and enhance public awareness of its plans for consequence analyses. These intentions were qualified, however, by the limited internal resources available for such programs and by the SEC's uncertainty as to how some of its rules could be monitored. It accordingly directed the Division of Corporate Finance to increase its monitoring activities and the Directorate of Economic and Policy Research to assist in remaining abreast of academic research. The sincerity of the SEC's intentions is demonstrated by its plans to hold public hearings on the impact of disclosure requirements on small businesses. The potential exists for feedback from the business community to impact SEC regulations. Even more important, however, will be the modification of reporting requirements in response to management's experiences.

Ex post consequence analysis ultimately involves stabilization of a change ensuring compliance with the reporting standard in the absence of influence from the policy setter. The FASB and SEC should ask whether their policy directives would be followed even if formal requirements were repealed. This goal necessitates creating a positive attitude toward the innovation and developing the technical ability of the business community to deal with the change in the absence of the policy maker.

SUMMARY

In building a framework for the resolution of accounting controversies, a sociological perspective was described wherein the economic consequences of accounting standards to all sectors of society was seen as important. Management's responsibility for financial reporting and reactions to disclosure requirements emerged as critical elements. Accounting policy was depicted as a plan for social change in which the policy board functioned as a change agent and the business community as a change target. The imposition of new reporting practices was described as an innovation invoking support or resistance by corporate management.

Because the accounting policy maker functions as a change agent, the process pursued to enact changes in reporting practices could be assessed as a program for planned social change. Six elements were seen as critical to the framework for enhancing the acceptability of a new accounting standard. First was the establishment of the need for a change in reporting practices. While the policy board may take the initiative in identifying an area where change is desired, acceptance of a proposed solution is enhanced if management concurs with this need. A second important element was sanction by the business community of the FASB and SEC as change agents so that public confidence exists in the policy-making process.

Communication channels involving both transmission of the desired changes by the policy setter and consideration of management's reactions was an additional element. This communication process is augmented by establishing formal procedures for feedback from affected parties, such as allowing outside representatives to be members on policy boards. Fourth was the importance of giving full recognition to the norms and customs of the business community and the effect of a proposed change on these values. The final elements, a priori consequence analysis and post-implementation monitoring, have received increasing attention due to the emphasis on considering the economic consequences of policy directives.

Chapter 4

THE ROLE OF THE ACCOUNTING POLICY MAKER

The standard setter's functionality as a change agent is important to the success of engineering change in financial reporting practices. The sociological aspects of the policy maker's role are fundamental to the framework for establishing programs of planned social change through accounting policy and for remaining attuned to the economic consequences of reporting requirements. This chapter examines the power position of the policy maker, its influence on gaining acceptance of proposed changes by the business community, and the relationship between power positions when more than one policy maker is involved.

THE POWER POSITION OF ACCOUNTING POLICY SETTERS

The possession of authority to formulate accounting standards is important since significant influence is then wielded over the corporate disclosure system. The extent of this influence depends on the power base from which the standard setter operates.

Types of power bases

A power position is defined as the relationship between the change agent and the target. Five such bases have been identified: (1) reward power in which the target perceives the agent as able to grant rewards or withdraw punishments, (2) coercive power whereby the agent is perceived as able to enact punishment or withhold rewards, (3) legitimate power in which the target perceives the agent as holding a sanctioned right to prescribe behavior, (4) referent power whereby the target identifies with the agent, and (5) expert power whereby the target perceives the agent as possessing some special knowledge or expertise (French and Raven 1960, pp. 612–613). Programs for planned changes in reporting practices by the FASB and SEC are influenced by the policy board's power position vis-à-vis the business community.

An important relationship exists between legitimate and coercive power. The target may view the change agent as using coercion in an area where there is not a legitimate right to threaten punishment. While the coercive nature of the power will most likely compel the target to implement the change, attitudinal acceptance may not be forthcoming, the agent's image may be damaged, and resistance to the agent's power and the innovation may arise. Coupling power with legitimacy yields authority, and if a coercive base is not seen as legitimate within the area of attempted influence, resistance and aversion to the change agent may intensify.

The coercive power of the SEC

The SEC acquired coercive power over firms governed by its filing requirements through Congressional authority granted in the 1933 and 1934 Acts. As quoted below, Section 19(a) of the Securities Act of 1933 gives the SEC authority to set forth the forms, rules, procedures, regulations, and all other requirements it deems necessary to ensure full and fair corporate disclosure:

> . . . shall have authority . . . to prescribe the form or forms in which required information shall be set forth, the items or details to be shown in the balance sheet and earning statement, and the methods to be followed in the preparation of accounts, in the appraisal or valuation of assets and liabilities, in the determination of depreciation and depletion, in the differentiation of recurring and nonrecurring income, in the differentiation of investment and operating income, and in the preparation, where the Commission deems it necessary or desirable, of consolidated balance sheets or income accounts . . . (as quoted by Skousen 1976, p. 86).

Under Section 13(b) of the Securities Exchange Act of 1934 this power was broadened to include periodic filing by registrants:

> The Commission may prescribe, in regard to reports made pursuant to this title, the form or forms in which the required information shall be set forth, the items or details to be shown in the balance sheet and the earning statement, and the methods to be followed in the preparation of

reports, in the appraisal or valuation of assets and liabilities, in the determination of depreciation and depletion, in the differentiation of recurring and nonrecurring income, in the differentiation of investment and operating income, and in the preparation, where the Commission deems it necessary or desirable, of separate and/or consolidated balance sheets or income accounts . . . (as quoted by Skousen 1976, p. 87).

The 1933 and 1934 Acts prescribe heavy responsibilities for the information disclosed on the management of firms whose stock is publicly traded. The SEC has devised well-established procedures for monitoring compliance with its reporting requirements pursuant to management's obligations. The Division of Corporate Finance is responsible for reviewing all registration statements by scrutinizing financial information for any material untrue, incomplete, or misleading disclosures. If deficiencies are found, a letter of comments is sent to the corporation requesting revision of the registration statement. Most often the company will comply by filing an amended statement.

Management may not concur with the SEC's comments, thus initiating a series of conferences between the firm and the SEC, in which the Office of Chief Accountant acts as mediator for any unresolved controversies. Although infrequently used, firms do have the ultimate right to appeal to the Commission itself. Failure to comply with the SEC's final decision by the corporation leaves three options. First, the deficient registration statement can be allowed to become effective, exposing management to legal liability for the disclosure of misleading information. Second, the SEC may issue a refusal order, whereby the registration statement is blocked from becoming effective. Third, a stop order may be issued either before or after the effective date, as in deficient filings under the 1934 Act. This technique precludes further consideration of the filing or discontinues trading in the security.

While there is no public record regarding the extent of noncompliance by corporations and punitive actions taken by the SEC, recourse to measures as strong as the stop order are seldom necessary. This is because firms wishing to initiate or retain public trading of their securities have little alternative but to follow the SEC's requirements, thus further strengthening the SEC's coercive power. The business community's perception of the legitimacy of the SEC for creating disclosure requirements is still an important factor, however, since it influences the SEC's authority position. For example, erosion in the SEC's power base occurred subsequent to ASR No. 190 which mandated the disclosure of replacement costs. Aversion to both the directive and the SEC arose, with critics asserting that the requirement represented an enlargement of the SEC's traditional "watchdog" role and "activism at its worst" (Carlson 1977; Bastable 1977).

The legitimate power of the FASB

The power base of the private-sector policy board has evolved largely in response to demands from the public sector. (See Zeff (1973) and Moonitz (1974) for an extensive treatment of the history of policy setting in the private sector.) Prior to 1938, the underlying philosophy of the American Institute of Accountants (predecessor to the AICPA) was that corporations should have flexibility and freedom to choose accounting principles. This conflicted with the desires of the SEC, which wanted the number of alternative accounting practices reduced. In 1938, the SEC issued ASR No. 4, stating in part:

> In cases where financial statements filed with this Commission pursuant to its rules and regulations under the Securities Act of 1933 or the Securities Exchange Act of 1934 are prepared in accordance with accounting principles for which there is no substantial authoritative support, such financial statements will be presumed to be misleading or inaccurate despite disclosures contained in the certificate of the accountant or in footnotes to the statements provided the matters involved are material (SEC 1938).

It soon became obvious that if the accounting profession did not take the initiative in establishing generally accepted accounting principles, the SEC would. Through the SEC's actions, the AICPA acquired more authority than it desired or with which it was prepared to deal. It responded by creating the CAP, composed solely of representatives from large CPA firms. During its twenty-year life, the CAP promulgated standards through Accounting Research Bulletins (ARB). The authority of these statements rested solely on their general acceptability, thus becoming standards only by consensus. Without power to require their use in practice even by AICPA members, acceptance of ARBs relied upon the persuasiveness of their logic and the support of agencies with coercive power such as the SEC and the New York Stock Exchange.

In 1959, a reorganization within the accounting profession resulted in the establishment of the APB. The new board lost a great deal of credibility early in its life following its confrontation with the SEC and Congress over the accounting treatment of the investment tax credit. Recognizing the need for additional authoritative power, in 1964 the Council of the AICPA passed a resolution as an appendix to APB Opinion No. 6, requiring disclosure of deviations from APB opinions. Generally accepted accounting principles were defined as those with substantial authoritative support and APB opinions were deemed constituting substantial authoritative support. Failure to disclose departures from APB opinions was judged substandard reporting coming under the purview of the AICPA's Practice Review Committee. No longer solely dependent upon general acceptance, the status of the APB's promulgations was accordingly raised. By the end of its life, respect for the APB had ebbed due to the extensive attention in the financial press given to accounting abuses and the problems of the APB in formulating standards. The support of the SEC did, however, enhance the authority of the APB opinions.

With the establishment of the FASB in 1972, several changes were made intended to strengthen the private sector's authority in setting accounting policy. First, the tripartite organization encompassed a broader representation of interests and it existed independent of the AICPA. By stipulating that three out of the seven FASB members could come from outside the public accounting profession, CPAs assumed a less dominant role in the standard-setting function. This wider participation was intended to increase the credibility of the FASB's promulgations.

A second bolster to the FASB's power came with a vote of support from the AICPA in 1972. In amending its Code of Professional Ethics, Rule 203 was adopted requiring CPAs to disclose all deviations from generally accepted accounting principles:

> A member shall not express an opinion that financial statements are presented in conformity with generally accepted accounting principles if such statements contain any departure from an accounting principle promulgated by the body designated by Council to establish such principles which has a material effect on the statements taken as a whole ... (AICPA 1972).

The AICPA Council later stated that generally accepted accounting principles were determined by the directives of the FASB. Significantly, failure to comply with FASB standards became a breach of ethics, subject to disciplinary action as severe as expulsion from the AICPA. Adoption of a resolution by the AICPA's governing council under Rule 204 of the Code of Professional Ethics represents the most recent support to the FASB's authority. Passed in May, 1979, this resolution sanctioned the FASB as a legitimate body for issuing policy directives for supplemental disclosures occurring outside of financial statements.

In 1973, the SEC issued ASR No. 150, containing a strong vote of confidence in the FASB, thus providing an additional source of authority for its promulgations:

> Principles, standards, and policies promulgated by the FASB in its Statements and Interpretations will be considered by the Commission as having substantial authoritative support, and those contrary to such FASB promulgation will be considered to have no such support (SEC 1973).

Coupled with the statement in ASR No. 4 that financial disclosures in filings with the SEC are misleading or inaccurate if they deviate from accounting principles with substantial authoritative support, the SEC placed great credence in the FASB's ability to develop accounting standards.

While the SEC possesses the authority to prescribe reporting requirements governing financial disclosures pursuant to the 1933 and 1934 Acts, it has preferred to depend on the accounting profession to develop and set forth accounting standards. Several reasons have been advanced for the SEC's reliance on the private sector (Chatov 1975; pp. 175–183; SEC 1978b). The accounting profession has greater resources for developing reporting standards, with more technical expertise and awareness of emerging problems. The predominance of SEC members with legal backgrounds has also limited the policy board's ability for and interest in developing accounting principles. Retention of the standard-setting function by the private sector has been viewed as desirable for preventing the development of two sets of accounting principles, one each for publicly- and nonpublicly-owned firms.

Avoidance of the rule-making arena is consistent with the SEC's philosophy that it is administering disclosure statutes and should not be unduly concerned with specific measurement issues. Private-sector formulation of accounting standards has forestalled SEC conflict with the accounting profession and financial community. The delegation of authority reflects a basic preference in the U.S. society for self-regulation. Blatant disregard for public responsibility has usually been a prerequisite for a governmental agency to usurp the authority of the private sector. The recent investigations led by Representative Moss, the late Senator Metcalf, and Senator Eagleton have been founded on this very premise. Although the private-sector policy board was not convicted and did not lose any of its delegated power, the allegations had the effect of weakening its credibility.

Rather than exercise its Congressional authority, the SEC has preferred to intensify its oversight of the formulation of accounting standards in the private sector. This oversight entails monitoring FASB and AICPA projects through their reports, attending meetings and public hearings, participating on committees and task forces, and ensuring that the SEC's views on specific standards and interpretations are fully communicated and considered. If the SEC believes the private sector is not responding to a changing condition or emerging problem, an ASR may be released to promulgate an accounting practice or disclosure rule in that particular area. As a result of the recent Congressional investigations, the SEC also makes annual reports to Congress on the self-governing activities of the accounting profession.

Despite its delegated rule-making authority, the FASB lacks direct legislative authority granting it enforcement powers; thus it is fundamentally dependent on voluntary adherence to its directives. This heightens the importance of the process by which standards are developed to the ultimate acceptance of the rules. Skepticism of the process contributes to rejection of the product. Threats to the acceptability of the FASB's policies come from the potential for overturn by the SEC, Congress, or other government agencies and the potential of circumvention by the business community.

Without immediate ability to mediate punishments to management for noncompliance, the FASB operates from a legitimate power base in which the business community accepts the FASB as having authority to set accounting policy, largely because of the SEC's support. Enforcement of specific standards is dependent on the CPA's ability to persuade management to comply with the requirements and, if necessary, modify the financial statements. Coercion is missing, however, since the firm can issue financial reports with "unaccepted" accounting principles and at worst receive a qualified audit opinion. While the CPA can withdraw from the engagement and refuse to issue an opinion, this necessitates the incurrence of an economic sacrifice by the audit firm to ensure compliance with the accounting standards it is charged with enforcing (Sterling 1973). Management is then free to search for an audit firm less adamant in its compliance requirements.

Management generally emerges in a superior power position over the CPA profession (Goldman and Barlev 1974; Nichols and Price 1976). The benefits to the company from the services of any one particular auditor are lessened by the existence of other CPA firms, equally qualified to perform the same functions. The benefits to the CPA firm from a relationship with the company derive from the fees obtained from performance of the audit services. These rewards are directly dependent upon the specific auditor-firm relationship. The large number of alternatives available to management for obtaining an audit, coupled with the greater value placed by the CPA firm on the rewards from the company than placed by the company on the rewards from any one auditor, produce an asymmetrical pattern of dependency.

Disagreement with a CPA may encourage management to "shop" for an accounting firm more likely to concur with its reporting practices. While this has been an important avenue for firms to circumvent the stringent application of accounting standards in reports to the public, the SEC has enacted two requirements which curtail such tactics: (1) only unqualified audit reports are accepted in filings with the SEC, and (2) if a registrant changes CPA firms, it must file Form 8-K with the SEC within ten days of the month of the change, giving the reason for the switch. This latter requirement specifies that any accounting or auditing disagreements occurring within the previous two years must be disclosed and if the auditor disagrees with the disclosure, a separate statement from the CPA must be included. Other attempts to mitigate the power imbalance include requirements in the AICPA Professional Code of Ethics that a newly engaged auditor ascertain from the previous CPA why it was replaced, more extensive use of audit committees composed of outside board of director members with responsibility for engaging the auditor, increased uniformity in practices through accounting standards to lessen the pressure on CPAs arising from allowable accounting alternatives, and heightened legal liability to third parties to strengthen CPAs motivation to counteract management.

The lack of coercive power has been identified as a major weakness in the operations of the FASB.

> ... the Achilles' heel of the FASB is its reliance on voluntary cooperation. ... Reliance on voluntary, willing "adherence" to the standards of an agency without explicit power of enforcement is illusory. Management will cooperate when it has no other choice, or when it suits its own goals and objectives, but not otherwise (Moonitz 1974, p. 87).

Suggestions for bolstering the FASB center on finding "allies" such as the SEC, stock exchanges, regulatory agencies, or major accounting organizations which would enforce the FASB's directives.

STRUCTURAL CONDITIONS OF POWER

In addition to the change agent's power base, two aspects of the change environment have been identified as determinants of the structural conditions of power (Warren 1968, pp. 954-957). First is the type of control sought by the policy maker: attitudinal conformity with inculcation of norms, or behavioral conformity through overt compliance without value acceptance. Second is the type of visibility or surveillance of conformity: low visibility when monitoring actions is difficult, or high visibility when compliance is easily observed. These structural conditions are related to the five power bases in Figure 4-1.

When change is engineered from a legitimate power base, a fairly high level of attitudinal conformity accompanied by internalization of values usually results. This is due to acceptance of the change agent's authority to prescribe behavior. A moderate amount of visibility is postulated as necessary, however, to ensure continued compliance with the prescriptions, since the standard setter's power tenuously relies on general acceptability.

The AICPA's Code of Professional Ethics and the SEC's ASR No. 150 indirectly encourage attitudinal conformity by the business community with the FASB's financial reporting requirements. This influence comes through acceptance of the promulgations by the accounting profession and the firm's CPAs. Surveillance of compliance is important; rather than monitoring financial reporting practices

Figure 4-1
Relationship between power bases, conformity, and visibility

Conformity	Power Base	Visibility
Behavioral	---------- Coercive Power ----------	High
	------------ Reward Power ------------	
	Expert Power Legitimate Power	
	Legitimate Power Expert Power	
	---------- Referent Power ----------	
Attitudinal		Low

directly, the accounting profession relies on sanctions to CPAs for a breach of ethics from deviant behavior. In essence, CPAs are given the task of policing the adherence of the business community to reporting standards.

This informal program for surveillance may be circumvented by corporate management. An example based on one research study is accounting for mergers pursuant to APB Opinions No. 16 and 17 (Gagnon 1971). These standards were intended to reduce the number of mergers treated as a pooling of interest. However, the implementation guidelines in the directives were complicated and arbitrary. Many borderline cases may have arisen in which CPAs felt justified in using pooling of interest to prevent risking the loss of a client. To some observers, the result was an erosion in the authority of the standards. Low visibility and thus difficulty in detecting deviant behavior enabled the business community to in fact reject the reporting requirements.

A coercive power base, such as the SEC's, results in high behavioral conformity but low value acceptance. Indifference and alienation often accompany forced compliance, and removal of the coercive mechanism can result in nondisclosure of much of the required information. This power base necessitates high surveillance due to the lack of attitudinal conformity. The Division of Corporate Finance accordingly reviews all filings, in contrast to the FASB which has no formal surveillance procedure. Additionally, no voluntary visible expression of acceptance of the SEC's authority exists, such as the AICPA Code of Professional Ethics. Given the coercive nature of this power base, such expressions are unnecessary for achieving conformity.

THE RELATIONSHIP BETWEEN THE FASB AND SEC

The effectiveness of a policy board cannot be assessed without considering its authority vis-à-vis other standard setters. This relationship involves not only the formal boundaries that establish spheres of authority, but also informally-evolved power relationships. The existence of two or more standard setters creates the potential for clashes over the resolution of controversial issues.

Relative power positions

The interaction between the FASB and the SEC influences the business community's perception of their relative power to establish accounting policy. Attempts have been made to limit the domain of each policy board. The FASB is purportedly concerned with measurement issues or the process of accumulating accounting data, while the SEC is involved with disclosure policy or the communication of information to external users. This distinction has never been workable, however, as the measurement and disclosure of financial information are not separable processes. The FASB (1978d, p. 3) recently stated that its activities encompass the larger field of financial reporting and are not restricted to the contents of financial statements. This broader role is interpreted as including financial information disclosed outside the financial statements, and nonfinancial disclosures such as narrative analyses (Carmichael 1979). With expanded boundaries, the FASB has moved to formulate requirements for supplemental disclosures such as inflation-accounting information. At the same time, the SEC has been concerned with measurement issues, as when it became involved in accounting for the investment tax credit and marketable securities.

Clearly the FASB and SEC operate within the same general territory: establishing financial accounting standards for use by corporations in external reporting. While formally it appears that the SEC has abdicated its standard-setting authority to the FASB, in reality the public sector still possesses significant influence over the establishment of accounting policy. The SEC's statutory authority for creating disclosure requirements, and the FASB's dependency on the SEC for its delegated authority, has led some to describe the institutional setting as an informal decentralized organizational structure (Horngren 1972, 1973; Rappaport 1977, p. 89). The ultimate authority for establishing financial reporting requirements rests with Congress, which must remain responsive to those parties most likely to be affected, generally financial statement users and preparers. This power has been entrusted to the SEC, which in turn has delegated its standard-setting authority to the private sector. Analogous to decentralization in an industrial setting, the SEC is depicted as the top management and the FASB as lower management.

Within this environment, the SEC is responsible for establishing overall policies and constraints on acceptable policy actions, as well as retaining ultimate veto power. Its involvement in the FASB's activities depends upon the extent of decentralization within the system. Generally, the private sector has been allowed to formulate and implement accounting standards. This arrangement has evolved from the accounting profession's greater resources, knowledge, experience, and abilities for resolving technical accounting issues. As a result, no one policy board possesses both the technical ability regarding accounting issues and the social legitimacy regarding public welfare issues. As the authority to create accounting requirements is delegated down the hierarchy, it is moved to those organizations with greater amounts of professional expertise, but less authority for social-welfare decisions.

A benefit to the SEC from this arrangement comes from the buffer role of the private sector. Interested parties outside the system are more likely to apply pressure on the FASB because it is more visibly involved in the creation of financial reporting directives. The SEC can portray its role as enforcing the standards established in the private sector. The shifting of this responsibility must be done carefully, however, for outsiders will appeal to higher levels of management: to the SEC for complaints regarding the FASB, and to Congress for criticisms of the SEC. In the short run, Congress may take no action if it decides the arrangement is adequate. But Congress will remain sensitive to the possibility that continued dissatisfaction by the public could result in political losses, such that in the long run outside pressure may affect accounting policies.

The dependence of power bases on delegation of authority within such a decentralized organization was discounted by former SEC Chief Accountant John C. Burton. He described the relationship as a partnership within an atmosphere of mutual nonsurprise, where each policy board is kept fully apprised of the other's actions. Rather than viewing the SEC as possessing absolute authority and the FASB as subservient to it, Burton (1973a, p. 26) believed that authority exists for both organizations, asserting the following: "We would believe it to be immoral if the APB or the FASB were a straw man behind which we would act as an *eminence grise*." (See also Burton 1973b.) The process of taking positions adversary to the FASB was described by Burton as a negative sum game, a game theory situation yielding a negative total payoff.

The critical element in Burton's conception of the interrelationship between the FASB and SEC is precisely how "mutual nonsurprise" is to be accomplished. In the past, cooperation and communication between the two groups has relied on informal networks; for example, by the assignment of a specific FASB member to direct liasion duties with the SEC. The lack of a formal mechanism to ensure each policy board remains fully informed on current deliberations inhibits awareness and sensitivity to each other's actions. The SEC, however, has become more directly involved in the FASB's activities as a part of its oversight of private-sector standard setting.

Some critics of the SEC's operations have claimed that it is actually the private sector that possesses the greatest power to formulate accounting standards (Chatov 1975, pp. 250–253, 262–264). Termed a role reversal, an authority relationship results such that the SEC relies on the FASB for guidance. Sporadic involvement of the SEC in the private-sector's activities is described as a threat ritual such that issues which develop into major controversies involving many vociferous outside interests evoke threats by the SEC for action if the private sector remains unresponsive. Allegedly, the purpose of this maneuver is to allow the standard-setting function to remain in the private sector while the SEC masks its eroding authority. Because the SEC does not intend to take the initiative in establishing generally accepted accounting principles, with a few specific exceptions, it becomes an "onlooker" in the overall process of formulating financial reporting standards.

Recent power struggles

It is difficult to form generalizations regarding the relationship between the private- and public-sector policy boards. A realistic assessment of the dynamics does not reveal consistent dominance of one group over the other. Instead, it appears that when both parties become interested in a particular issue the ensuing events result in a power struggle, and the ultimate outcome depends not only on which policy board dominates, but also on the other outside pressures involved. Two recent events have demonstrated that the power relationships are complex: oil and gas accounting and inflation accounting.

In passing the Energy Policy and Conservation Act of 1975, Congress charged the SEC with prescribing uniform accounting procedures for use by oil and gas producers in reporting data to the Department of Energy. Consistent with its preference for private-sector development of accounting standards, the SEC entrusted this assignment to the FASB. Following two years of research, the FASB issued an exposure draft in July, 1977. Mandatory use of the successful efforts method of accounting for exploration, development, and production costs was proposed, such that all costs of nonproducing wells would be treated as current period expenses. The full-cost method, allowing for capitalization and subsequent amortization of costs for both successful and unsuccessful ventures, would be prohibited. In August, 1977, the SEC issued a release stating it intended to support the conclusions reached by the FASB in its exposure draft. FAS No. 19 was issued in December, 1977, with only minor changes from the provisions in the exposure draft.

The elimination of full-cost accounting as an accepted accounting practice incited widespread opposition by firms then using the method, mostly small independent oil and gas companies. General criticism related to the ability of firms to manipulate profits through the timing of exploration activities. More serious allegations focused on the negative impact successful efforts would have on earnings, reducing profits and net worth below what they would be under full costing, thus purportedly inhibiting the ability of smaller companies to raise capital. The expectation of such negative results would discourage aggressive exploration efforts and decrease competition in the oil industry.

The ensuing controversy prompted the Department of Energy to hold hearings in February, 1978, primarily to assess the impact of requiring successful efforts accounting on the U.S. energy supply and to formulate a recommendation for action by the SEC. Assertions that FAS No. 19 would be anticompetitive led the Department of Justice to request that the SEC hold hearings to demonstrate otherwise, and to mandate that the SEC choose the least anticompetitive method. This situation provided a ready excuse for the SEC if it decided to reject the FASB's directive; modifications to the private-sector's rule could be made under the guise of maintaining competition.

Succumbing to the pressures from small independent producers with strong vested interests and the concerns of other governmental agencies, the SEC decided against the mandatory use of successful efforts. In ASR No. 253 issued in August, 1978, the SEC stated that neither successful-efforts nor full-cost accounting provide adequate information. It therefore proposed to develop a current value method, reserve recognition accounting, allowing for recognition of the value of reserves as income when proved, and exploration and development costs as expenses when incurred. Disclosure requirements were issued governing the transition to the new method, and either successful-efforts or full-cost accounting would be accepted in the interim.

The SEC stressed that by preempting FAS No. 19, it was not modifying its stance toward the private-sector's role in formulating accounting standards. The situation that developed concerning oil and gas accounting was viewed by the SEC as unique, and the rejection of the FASB's directive was considered an exception to the SEC's preference for standard setting in the private sector. While the SEC emphasized its actions related solely to substantive issues of oil and gas accounting, it also strongly reiterated in ASR No. 253 its fundamental authority to create financial reporting requirements:

> The Commission's policy recognized that the FASB operates to establish accounting standards, but it does not involve a delegation of the Commission's substantive rulemaking authority to the FASB. While the Commission recognizes that, in general, it is most desirable for the private sector rather than the government to develop accounting standards, the Commission retains the final authority under the federal securities laws to promulgate rules, including financial accountings standards, that govern the preparation and presentation of financial statements issued by publicly owned companies, regardless of the FASB's determinations (SEC 1978c).

The Trustees of the FAF attempted to clarify the implications of the SEC's actions by emphasizing the extraordinary nature of the situation:

> While some may view the Commission's actions as signaling important differences between the FASB and the Commission in terms of resolving substantial accounting issues, SEC Chairman Harold M. Williams assures us such is not the case and happened in this situation only because of the uniqueness of the oil and gas matter (FASB 1978b).

Despite these assertions, the SEC's move was taken as initial indications of eroding support for the FASB's ability to formulate accounting standards. Through suggesting the use of an accounting procedure not seriously considered by the private sector, the SEC limited its rejection of the FASB's promulgation. More significantly, however, this situation represented the first break of the SEC from an FASB policy.

The SEC's action created a serious conflict between the reporting requirements for oil and gas companies of the SEC and FASB. Companies not registered with the SEC, primarily small independent producers, would be required to use successful efforts accounting pursuant to FAS No. 19. Publicly held companies would be allowed to prepare financial reports for the SEC using either full-cost or successful efforts. Yet the use of the full-cost method for annual reports to shareholders by those same firms would necessitate a qualified audit report for deviation from FAS No. 19. The FASB's solution for eliminating this contradiction was to issue FAS No. 25, indefinitely suspending the December 15, 1978, effective date of FAS No. 19. The discrepancy in reporting requirements may have given the FASB an excuse for backing down from the SEC without too much damage to its credibility. Indeed, the FASB could have completely relented by rescinding FAS No. 19. By retaining the substance of the standard, however, the policy board was remaining firm in its preference for successful efforts accounting.

The events which surrounded the formulation of accounting standards for the oil and gas industry clearly illustrate the importance of sociological and political factors in the creation of policy. Consistent with its user orientation and the tenets espoused in FAC No. 1, the FASB asserted that the risk and uncertainty associated with exploration costs were too great to justify their capitalization as assets. Current expensing of these costs as required by the FASB would have a negative impact on the earnings report of a large number of oil and gas producers. Outside parties appealed to governmental agencies using public interest arguments such as anticompetitiveness and detrimental impact on allocation of capital. These agencies accordingly charged the SEC with responsibility for considering such arguments.

A power struggle developed between the FASB advocating the needs of financial statement users, and the SEC feeling pressure from financial statement preparers with vested interests and governmental agencies with social-welfare concerns. The result was inevitable. To forestall eventual criticism by higher authorities, the SEC was forced to pull a power play on the FASB and exercise its ultimate authority to establish financial reporting standards.

Proposals for inflation accounting also illustrate the importance of the relationship between the FASB and SEC in finalizing disclosure requirements. The continuation of unabated inflation heightened the SEC's concern for the adequacy of financial reports prepared on the historical cost basis. It felt that financial statement users should be provided with information on the current costs of operating the business and the current economic investment in fixed assets and inventories. In March, 1976, ASR No. 190 was issued, requiring the supplemental disclosure of the current replacement cost of inventories and productive assets, and the impact on cost of sales and depreciation of using a current-cost basis. Vehement opposition to the directive arose from the companies forced to comply. Criticism centered on many aspects of the mandate: cost to prepare the data, uselessness of the disclosures, heavy reliance on subjective estimates, tenuous assumption of replacement of all assets, and incomplete disclosure of inflation effects due to omission of monetary gains and losses and operating cost savings.

Also concerned with the distorting impact of inflation, the FASB (1978e) issued an exposure draft in December, 1978, containing its proposal for supplemental disclosures. The FASB appeared cognizant of corporate opposition to ASR No. 190. Its proposal thus allowed for experimentation with one of two methods: a corporation could elect to present information regarding income from continuing operations on either a constant-dollar basis or a current-cost basis. By allowing for the use of general price level adjusted statements, the FASB was retaining the historical cost basis of accounting and forestalling complaints that the resulting disclosures would be judgmental and subjective.

Current-cost disclosures apply to property, plant and equipment, inventories, depreciation expense, and cost of goods sold. The assets subject to revaluation were only those actually owned, not those theoretically acquired as replacements. This eliminated objections to the SEC's requirements which necessitate unrealistic assumptions of replacement. Computation of current cost would proceed using replacement cost, net realizable value, or value in use, thus allowing for flexibility in determining the appropriate measurement. All firms were to be required to disclose, separate from income from continuing operations, gains or losses on net monetary items due to inflation and foreign exchange gains or losses. Complaints relating to the partial nature of disclosures pursuant to ASR No. 190 thus would not arise under the FASB's requirements.

This proposal gave rise to the potential for two contradictory reporting requirements. Firms reporting to the SEC would need to calculate the replacement cost of productive capacity and inventories. Nonpublicly owned companies, however, could make these supplemental disclosures under the FASB proposal using either general price level adjustments or the current costs of assets owned. As seen in the following quote from SEC Chairman Harold Williams (FASB 1979a), initial indications were that the SEC was supporting the FASB's actions:

> While we have not considered the current [FASB] exposure draft in depth, it appears to be a positive step forward in providing useful information concerning the effect of changing prices. If an appropriate final

standard is adopted by the Board concerning the effects of changing prices, I would expect the Commission to consider amending or rescinding its replacement cost rule in such a manner that registrants would be required to comply with the adopted exposure standards of the Board.

Concern emerged, however, that should the SEC accept the FASB's requirements as proposed, a lower standard of disclosure would result if most companies elected the constant-dollar alternative. Pressure on the FASB came from all sides: many of the comments to the exposure draft were in support of constant-dollar accounting, a significant minority favored current-cost disclosure, the SEC stood by its replacement-cost requirements, and the FASB itself was split on the issue ("Inflation Accounting: Nobody likes the FASB's New Approach—But What Else Is There?" 1979). It became evident to the FASB that the lack of consensus among its constituents and the futility of confronting the SEC precluded it from mandating one measurement scheme or allowing corporations a free choice. Rather than drop its involvement in inflation accounting, the FASB (1979d) decided to require supplemental disclosures on both a constant-dollar and current-cost basis. It considers these disclosure requirements experimental and educational, and it will monitor financial statement user reaction to determine the relative desirability of the methods.

There are subtle similarities between the formulation of rules for oil and gas accounting and inflation accounting. Contrary to the oil and gas situation, however, in inflation accounting the FASB appeared more attuned than the SEC to the vested interests of all the relevant parties. Reference to ASR No. 190 shows that the SEC's objective in requiring the disclosure of replacement costs was to enhance the adequacy of information to investors, or a user orientation. Objections from corporate management not wishing to disclose replacement costs were largely ignored.

In devising its requirements, the FASB attempted to remain sensitive to a broader base of outside pressures. Corporate complaints to the provisions of ASR No. 190 were studied to avoid such shortcomings in the FASB's directive. Attempts to satisfy the desires of both the business community and SEC led to a multiple-disclosure requirement for what is termed a period of experimentation. This complexity clearly detracts from the utility of the information; thus it does not appear that the FASB adopted a pure user orientation to resolving the problem of inflation accounting. While the FASB has demonstrated greater awareness of the socio-political nature of its job, whether it will be able to adequately satisfy all its constituents in devising inflation-accounting requirements remains to be seen.

SUMMARY

The effectiveness of the standard setter's change program was seen as influenced by the power relationship between the policy board and the business community. The SEC possesses coercive power, arising from its Congressional authority to establish financial reporting standards. The FASB depends on legitimate power from authority delegated by the SEC and from general public acceptance. Attitudinal versus behavioral conformity and the visibility of deviant actions are structural conditions related to the policy setter's power base.

The relative power between the FASB and SEC suggests that the FASB ultimately may be dependent on the SEC for its authority. Recent issues have demonstrated that the interactions are complex. While the SEC usurped the FASB in establishing reporting standards for oil and gas producers, the FASB has attempted to forestall a repeat of this situation by remaining more attuned to its constituents' and the SEC's desires for inflation accounting.

Chapter Five

STRATEGIES FOR PROMULGATING ACCOUNTING STANDARDS

The appropriate strategy for enacting change and gaining acceptance of a new standard depends on the power relationship between the policy maker and the business community, the behavioral and/or attitudinal conformity sought, and the extent to which noncompliance is visible. Strategies involve general plans for engineering change, while tactics refer to detailed steps for accomplishing the overall strategy. The purpose of this chapter is to consider the different strategies used by accounting policy makers in the private and public sectors. An examination of various financial reporting issues and their resolution by policy boards illustrates the types of strategies which have been used and their success.

TYPES OF STRATEGIES

Three general types of change strategies exist, relating to the change agent's power base and the structural conditions of that power (Kotler 1972, pp. 183–184; Chin and Benne 1972, pp. 234–235). First, persuasion, or an empirical-rational strategy, stresses the innovation's compatibility with the business community's existing value scheme and focuses on demonstrating the desirability and beneficial aspects of the change. Education, or a normative-reeducation strategy, is a second approach in which attitudinal conformity is sought through attempts to modify management's beliefs, attitudes, and values. This strategy extends beyond persuasion as it encompasses more than just knowledge and rational acceptance of an innovation. Finally, coercion or a power strategy involves the use of punishments and rewards to secure behavioral compliance. Altering management's value scheme receives secondary importance, as punishment is mediated for lack of overt behavioral changes. If a coercive power base exists, the change target may invite the use of power by ignoring persuasion or education strategies.

The innovation adoption decision made in a coercive situation differs from that following the use of persuasion or education. In all three strategies, the need for a change and the suggested solution are proposed by the policy maker. If persuasion or education are used to encourage change by the business community, the decision whether to adopt or reject the innovation is ultimately made by management. In a coercive strategy, however, it is the change agent who decides if the innovation is to be implemented. Communication of the desired change will be affected by the strategy; convincing arguments will be necessary if management makes the adoption decision, while compliance requirements will be emphasized if the change is mandated. Implementation of the innovation is more probable with coercion. However, overt behavioral modification does not imply that the target agrees with the change agent's adoption decision or that attitudinal acceptance will materialize.

Accounting policy makers have used all three strategies in the endeavor to gain acceptance of reporting standards. The importance of employing the most appropriate strategy to encourage acceptance of change and a particular standard was stressed in the following description of the APB:

> Perhaps the APB should really be renamed as the Accounting Principles-Political Action Board. Without public support, which usually means without the widespread support of industry, significant changes are seldom possible. Perhaps the situation would be better expressed negatively. If there is widespread hostility to a suggested accounting principle, there is small chance of implementing it—regardless of how impeccable its logic or how heavy the support within the Board (Horngren 1972, pp. 39–40; see also 1973).

Thus the marketing of accounting policy, or the use of strategies and tactics which enhance both attitudinal and behavioral acceptance, is at least as important as the technical assessment of which accounting method should be chosen.

The determination of a functional strategy is critically dependent on the characteristics of the social system (Warren 1968). Where there is a high degree of professionalism such as in the accounting environment, referent, expert, and legitimate power coupled with persuasion and education usually result in greater acceptance of the innovation since attitudinal congruence is emphasized. Coercive and reward power, as used in coercive strategies, focus on behavioral conformity and are usually more effective in a nonprofessional environment. A professional's proclivity for value compatibility culminating in attitudinal conformity, and the ineffectiveness of coercive strategies for achieving a change in covert states, lessens the chances for successful change without some utilization of persuasion or education.

STRATEGIES USED IN THE PRIVATE SECTOR

Lacking coercive power, policy makers in the private sector have been forced to experientially discover which strategies are most functional in gaining acceptance of directives. Interference from other policy agencies such as the SEC and Congress has influenced the evolution of strategies employed.

The APB

Dissatisfaction with the progress of the CAP led the AICPA Executive Committee to appoint a Special Committee on Research Program, charged with preparing a recommendation of the AICPA's role in establishing accounting principles (Zeff 1972, pp. 167–173). The Committee issued its report in 1958, in which it proposed the creation of the APB. The function of this new policy board was to formulate generally accepted accounting principles and reduce the number of differing and inconsistent accounting practices. Notably, the Committee stated that the APB was to rely on persuasion rather than compulsion in achieving these objectives. The tone was thus set for the APB as it embarked on demonstrating that its standards were desirable in a normative sense, representing good financial reporting practices.

Soon after its foundation, the APB became embroiled in the investment tax credit controversy, and it learned firsthand that issuing directives founded on economic-reality arguments and relying on a persuasive strategy was a naive and unworkable approach. (See Zeff (1972, pp. 178–180) and Moonitz (1966, 1974, pp. 47–49) for a history of the investment tax credit controversy.) Following the proposal in Congress of legislation to enact an investment tax credit, the APB became involved in the accounting treatment of the tax reduction. An exposure draft was issued by the APB calling for uniform usage of the deferral method, spreading the tax benefit over the life of the property. Significant controversy ensued; the business community objected to the mandatory use of the deferral method, the SEC stated it might not support the exclusive use of one method, and governmental officials wishing to shore up a waning economy were vitally concerned with the outcome. Most critics preferred that the flow-through method be allowed, so that the entire tax benefit could directly reduce current taxes in the year of the credit.

Despite this known opposition, APB Opinion No. 2 was issued in 1962 mandating the use of the deferral method. Within a few days, after four major accounting firms announced they would not follow the directive, the SEC issued ASR No. 96, stating that both the deferral and flow-through methods were acceptable practices for use in filings by registrants. Philip L. Defliese (1979), past chairman of the APB, notes that the SEC statement was a last minute "waffle." While the Chief Accountant favored the deferral method, pressure from the government on the SEC Chairman resulted in acceptance of the flow-through method. This action effectively nullified the APB's directive, and in 1964 APB Opinion No. 4 was issued, allowing the use of either method in accounting for the investment tax credit.

Unfortunately this controversy was reopened in 1971 when Congress began deliberations to reinstate the investment tax credit. The APB issued an exposure draft proposing mandatory use of the deferral method, having first secured the concurrence of the Department of the Treasury and the SEC. Corporate pressure soon mounted on Congress to retain flexibility in accounting methods. The bill as passed by Congress prohibited any taxpayer from being required to use a particular accounting method for the investment tax credit.

Because it represented a novel situation, the APB was not confined to choosing from methods already used in practice. Instead it had a "golden opportunity" to establish a new principle. Viewed theoretically, the appropriate treatment of the investment tax credit largely involves conceptual issues with few pragmatic problems. As the APB learned, however, seeking a normative solution while ignoring the vested interests of the business community and the goals of the federal government enhances rejection of the solution. The critical issue may have been whether the APB could continue to rely solely on persuasion, or whether its directives needed compulsion to increase the APB's authority (Zeff 1972, pp. 180–182). The AICPA agreed that the APB's power needed strengthening and began requiring the disclosure of deviations from APB opinions.

Beginning in 1968, the APB again embarked on a program of persuasion, this time attempting to convince the business community not to use pooling of interests to account for mergers. As the merger movement gained momentum in the 1960s, criteria for distinguishing between a pooling of interest and a purchase type of business combination became unclear (Zeff 1972, pp. 212-216). The subject captured the interest of the financial press, SEC, Federal Trade Commission, Congressional committees, government officials, FEI, and financial executives.

Under pressure from the SEC to provide guidelines to reduce the diversity of practices and alleged abuses, the APB created a subject area committee to study the issue. Several point outlines were issued, and a public hearing was held to solicit outsiders' views. An exposure draft of an opinion was issued in 1969, proposing to eliminate pooling as an acceptable practice. While the Federal Trade Commission supported this position, the FEI and some public accountants were fervently opposed. Opinion within the APB itself was sharply divided. A second symposium was held to consider the varied opinions, and a revised exposure draft was issued which retained pooling subject to a three-to-one size test. Since this provision severely restricted the use of pooling, the FEI remained opposed. Letters of comment were received from 860 parties, 90 percent of which objected to some aspect of the proposal. The SEC supported the APB's position, as did the New York and American Stock Exchanges. In a new proposal, the size test was modified to nine-to-one. Further compromises led to the final opinion which allowed the use of pooling under restricted circumstances, but not subject to a size test.

The APB's sensitivity to outside interests has been cited as an early example of economic impact analysis in the formulation of policy (Wyatt 1977, pp. 92-93). By 1970, an economic downturn was beginning. Compromise and relaxation of its stringent prohibitions against pooling enabled the APB to remain alert to the potential for detrimental effects on the merger movement and the capital accumulation process. While largely unsuccessful in securing corporate support for this proposal, the APB's attentiveness to the opinions of the various interested parties helped avoid the dire consequences experienced in the investment tax credit debacle. The controversy was also significant in the history of strategies used by the private sector. Subsequent to this experience, the APB ceased issuing standards on controversial or sensitive issues, focusing instead on topics resolved in earlier opinions, extensions of previous work, or solutions to immediate pragmatic problems (Moonitz 1974, p. 28). The change in emphasis was partially due to the advent of the FASB. But the APB also appeared to realize the political nature of its job, and the futility of attempting to gain acceptance of change solely on the basis of persuasion. This reality was addressed by the creators of the FASB through provisions to strengthen its authority.

THE FASB

Concurrent with the enhanced political awareness of the FASB was increased recognition that an education/experimentation strategy might facilitate gradual change. Tactics involved in this strategy emphasize modification of existing attitudes by exhorting corporate management to voluntarily acquire experience with an innovation.

The private sector's actions to deal with financial reporting in periods of inflation exemplify gradual inculcation of change. Attempts to alter the business community's deep-seated biases against deviations from a historical-cost basis for financial reporting have largely relied upon increasing its knowledge of and familiarity with alternative measurement models. (See FASB (1978e) for a complete background of the private-sector's involvement in inflation accounting.) Concern with the distorting effect of inflation on conventional financial statements had been expressed by both the CAP and APB. Prior to the 1960s, adjustments for price changes were limited to accelerated depreciation for long-lived assets and last-in, first-out valuation for inventories. These two procedures lowered reported earnings to approximate net income after allowing for the current costs of operations. More extensive adjustments were suggested in APB Statement No. 3. Issued in 1969, this statement recommended providing general price-level adjusted financial data as supplemental information to historical-cost financial statements. The suggestion was never formalized in an opinion, and few companies voluntarily reported such information.

The FASB first addressed the problems arising from inflation in 1974, with the issuance of a discussion memorandum suggesting mandatory disclosure of supplemental general price-level adjusted financial information. Following public hearings, at which most objections centered on the use of a general price-level index to make the adjustments, an exposure draft was issued at the end of 1974, proposing to require that supplementary financial information adjusted for general price-level changes be included in the firm's financial reports.

Letters of comment to the exposure draft were received from 476 interested parties. In late 1975, the FASB announced it was postponing final action so that it could give adequate consideration to the issues raised in the letters. Additionally, the FASB was interested in the results from two field tests of implementing the proposed requirements, one being conducted in eighty-four companies and a second in twenty petroleum firms. In 1976, the FASB again announced it was postponing final resolution, this time citing the pending development of a conceptual framework and the SEC's recently-issued requirements for the disclosure of replacement cost data. Suggesting the need for further education, the FASB also stated that neither financial statement preparers nor users had an adequate understanding of general price-level adjusted information to mandate disclosure. Given the current state of knowledge, the FASB was concerned that the costs of inflation-reporting requirements would exceed the benefits from such disclosures.

Shortly thereafter, a discussion memorandum emanating from the conceptual framework project was issued, focusing on the elements of financial statements and their measurement. Two public hearings were held at which the efficacy of inflation-adjusted financial statements was a major topic. In May, 1977, the results from the experimental implementation by 101 companies of the provisions in the 1974 exposure draft for the period 1972 to 1974 were published.

Considerable education and experimentation preceded the December, 1978, issuance of the FASB's exposure draft for a standard on financial reporting during periods of changing prices. Dual benefits were derived from this strategy. Not only did the business community gradually become familiar with the idea of and techniques for deviating from the historical-cost model, but the accounting profession discovered which alternatives gave rise to greatest opposition by the business community ("Inflation Accounting: The FASB Takes the Plunge" 1979). For example, in formulating its proposal, the FASB used the consumer price index for information prepared on a general purchasing power basis rather than the general price-level index, a requirement in the FASB's 1974 proposal which was severely criticized.

The SEC's requirements for replacement-cost disclosures provided an indirect program of experimentation for the FASB, since it was able to identify problem areas and avoid them in creating its own requirements. The hypothetical nature of the assumption of lump-sum replacement was avoided by requiring only the current cost of assets actually owned. Implementation experiences from the field tests undoubtedly shaped the operational aspects of provisions for constant-dollar disclosures. The modifications in the FASB's requirements represent the abandonment of normative arguments for general price-level adjusted information, largely due to reactions from the business community following its exposure to nontraditional measurement techniques. The programs of experimentation heightened management's awareness of the distorting effect of inflation and the alternative solutions, thus providing an important source of education for the business community.

Provisions contained within the FASB's 1978 proposal stressed experimentation with a variety of techniques. In its exposure draft, the FASB (1978e, p. ii) explicitly emphasized the importance of education for financial statement users and preparers, as well as policy setters, at this stage of development in accounting for changing prices:

> The measurement and reporting of information on changing prices will require a substantial learning process on the part of all concerned. The Board makes no pretense of having solved all of the implementation problems. Rather, it encourages experimentation within the guidelines of this Statement and the development of new techniques that fit the particular circumstances of the enterprise and of the user. The proposed Statement has been written to provide more flexibility than is customary in Board Statements, in the belief that those involved will help to develop techniques that further the understanding of the effects of price changes on the enterprise.

The flexibility largely resulted from the choice between supplemental information prepared using historical cost/constant-dollar accounting or current-cost accounting.

To address measurement problems unique to particular industries and develop possible solutions, the FASB appointed six task groups composed of experts from each sector: banking, forest products, insurance, mining, oil and gas, and real estate. Attempts to involve interested parties from these industries included separate public hearings held by each task group. A conference was sponsored by the FASB on the findings of these studies to enhance the understanding of both the need for and provision of inflation-adjusted financial information, and to give full consideration to the diverse viewpoints held by both financial statement users and preparers. Education was clearly important to the FASB in engineering movement away from sole reliance on historical-cost information. Even more significant, however, was the critical role corporate management, and its experiences with reporting inflation data, was accorded by the FASB.

Lacking coercive authority, the FASB is unable to use a power strategy without backing from a second party acting as an "ally." The critical nature of this relationship is exemplified by the events surrounding the creation of accounting standards for the oil and gas industry. The delegation of this responsibility from Congress to the SEC, and then to the FASB, meant that the FASB inherited coercive power over which accounting method was to be used. Support by the SEC for the provisions of FAS No. 19 would have resulted in implementation of the FASB's directive through coercion, as all oil and gas producers would have been forced to use successful-efforts accounting in reporting to the SEC and the Department of Energy. This backing was not forthcoming, however, and the FASB soon realized it was powerless to secure compliance with its standard. Rather than face further disgrace from blatant disregard of its policy, the FASB postponed the effective date of FAS No. 19.

STRATEGIES USED BY THE SEC

Possession of a significant amount of power by the SEC precludes the direct use of persuasion over the business community. Mention by the SEC of a preferred accounting alternative gives rise to thoughts by management of potential detrimental consequences from disregard of such preferences. The SEC has, however, used a persuasive strategy on private-sector policy boards. When an issue arises on which the SEC has an opinion but does not wish to issue a directive, it may attempt to convince the FASB of the merits of its preferred solution. By persuading the FASB to support its alternative, the SEC indirectly obtains compliance by the business community.

Deliberations over accounting for the marketable securities by the APB provide an example of the SEC's persuasive tactics (Horngren

1973). After three years of deliberations, an APB Subcommittee concluded in 1971 that the flow-through (market value) method should be adopted, where all realized and unrealized gains and losses from value changes in securities are recognized in the current period. The insurance industry violently opposed this proposal, and the SEC set out to convince the APB that the flow-through method was highly undesirable, even submitting a position paper to the APB. By 1972, the APB had dropped the topic because it was unable to obtain the required majority to issue a standard. The ability of the SEC to induce the APB away from an alternative so vehemently opposed by the business community may have forstalled pernicious consequences from insistence on the flow-through method.

It is difficult to deny the compelling nature of the SEC's desires upon the business community. The SEC's power position significantly strengthens its influence. This is not a recent phenomenon. Early in its history the SEC attempted to eliminate intangibles such as goodwill from registrants' balance sheets without issuing a directive banning the accounts (Rappaport 1972, p. 7.10). Pressure from the SEC was so great that firms removed the intangibles so that their registration statements would become effective without delay.

The SEC's involvement in engineering changes in financial reporting practices has encompassed varying degrees of activism. Education and experimentation have been used functionally by the SEC to gradually gain acceptance of an innovation, as in product-line reporting and forecasting. Concern with the intensity of the merger movement of the 1960s prompted a Senate Subcommittee to consider the merits of segment reporting to facilitate antitrust investigations. (For a discussion of the events surrounding product-line reporting, see Skousen (1976) and Zeff (1972, pp. 202–204).) By 1966 the SEC had become interested in product-line reporting by diversified companies and appeared ready to present new disclosure requirements. At the request of the FEI, it agreed to delay any proposals until the FEI's research division was able to complete a study of the issues. This began two years of extensive research and experimental implementation by not only the FEI, but also the NAA and APB. As a result of this wide involvement in studying the efficacy of product-line reporting, the business community became aware of line-of-business reporting, its computation, uses, problem areas, and advantages.

After giving full consideration to the research findings, the SEC issued a proposal in 1968 to extend the disclosures of diversified companies. The proposal was revised in light of the comments received, and in 1969 regulations were adopted requiring supplemental product-line disclosures. Corporate acceptability of this innovation was fostered by the SEC's sensitivity to the views of interested parties, and its full cooperation with outside groups concerned with segment reporting. Attempts by the SEC to gain corporate understanding and approval prior to issuance of the final standard enhanced attitudinal as well as behavioral acceptance of the requirements when compliance was finally mandated.

The period of research and public discussion regarding product-line disclosures fulfilled an important educational purpose for the business community. The requirements as adopted, however, continued the learning and experimentation process through broad and flexible guidelines giving management considerable discretion in resolving implementation issues. For example, precise criteria were not established defining lines of business. Instead, management was left to use its judgment to define those segments it considered most meaningful. Continued latitude in compliance lessened the magnitude of the change and facilitated ultimate acceptability of the innovation.

Until 1973, the SEC prohibited the inclusion of predictions of future economic performance in filings by registrants. The SEC gradually recognized that projections were widely used in investment decision making, but that investors did not have equal access to such information. In 1975 it proposed complicated rules, mandating the inclusion of projections in registration filings if such data were provided to any outside parties. Strong opposition to this proposal was voiced, with many corporate critics asserting they would cease issuing future projections to outsiders such as security analysts rather than comply with the SEC's reporting requirements. The SEC withdrew its initial proposal, and in 1976 replaced it with a rule stating that while it would not stand in the way of registrants choosing to include projections in filings, it would neither encourage nor discourage the disclosure of such forecasts. The suggestion for a safe-harbor rule was also withdrawn. Proposed guides for the disclosure of projections were concurrently issued, aimed at encouraging experimentation by retaining flexibility in the guidelines.

The SEC Advisory Committee on Corporate Disclosure (1977, pp. 344–365) considered the desirability and feasibility of reporting forward looking data, or "soft" information, by registrants. It recommended that the SEC issue a public statement to promote an experimental program for the discretionary disclosure of projections of future company economic performance. To enhance voluntary compliance, the Advisory Committee stressed that corporations should be accorded significant flexibility in the nature and extent of their projections. Contrary to the 1976 proposed guides, which indicated companies should at a minimum disclose forecasts of revenues or sales, net income, and earnings per share, the Advisory Committee recommended that corporations be given complete discretion in determining the items to be projected. The Advisory Committee also stressed the need for a safe-harbor rule, in place of relying on protection from the 1933 and 1934 Acts as had been suggested in the 1976 proposed guides.

The SEC concurred with the Advisory Committee's recommendations, and in 1978 adopted guidelines to foster corporate projections. Flexibility and voluntary compliance were stressed in the provisions. Attenuation to the severe opposition to required forecasts encouraged the SEC to adopt a strategy of gradual change and thus initiate a period of education and experimentation. The complexity of earlier rules and the rigidity from stipulating the types of data to be disclosed have also been avoided. Current guidelines leave to management's discretion the nature of the information included, forecast period, disclosure of assumptions, subsequent comparisons with actual results, updates to the projections, discontinuation and later resumption of forecasting, and third-party review. The SEC proposed a safe-harbor rule for corporations issuing projections, intended to lessen corporate resistance to forecasting by reducing potential liability for inaccurate projections. This latitude should give management ample opportunity to gain from experience with the public disclosure of forecasts, and thus enhance the possibility of acceptance of this innovation.

When first concerned with distortions from using historical cost for financial reporting in periods of inflation, the SEC adopted an education strategy for encouraging corporations to deviate from the traditional accounting model. In 1973, it issued ASR No. 151, exhorting registrants to report inventory profits arising from the difference between cost of goods sold measured using historical costs and current replacement costs. Few corporations chose to make these voluntary disclosures. The failure of this educational approach can be attributed to the unsuccessful demonstration to the business community of any benefits from disclosing the data, the lack of experimental implementation in corporations, and the paucity of research into the impact on information preparers and users from reporting replacement costs.

Disappointed with noncompliance to ASR No. 151, and convinced of investors' need for information regarding current operating costs, the SEC issued a release in 1975 proposing new rules for mandatory disclosure of replacement costs of inventories and productive capacity. Over 350 letters of comment to this proposal were received by the SEC, largely opposing the requirements. Yet early in 1976, the SEC proceeded to issue ASR No. 190, directing approximately 1,000 corporations to disclose the current replacement cost of inventories and fixed assets, and the corresponding effect on cost of goods sold and depreciation, in their annual filings with the SEC. Instead of working with the business community to gain cooperation and attitudinal acceptance of the proposed change, as was done with line-of-business reporting, the SEC used its coercive power to compel a change in reporting practices.

The SEC's mandate for the disclosure of replacement costs exemplifies a coercive strategy and an authoritative innovation decision, in which the change was forced on the business community by a policy setter in a superior power position. The SEC took the initiative in identifying the need for a change in present financial reporting practices, inculcating this need in the business community, and formulating a solution to the problem. Both the accounting profession and corporate management have acknowledged the need for reporting the effect of inflation in the firm's financial statements (Corbin 1977; DeWelt 1977; Garsombke 1978). Extensive disagreement exists, however, over the appropriate method of disclosing the impact of price-level changes, and the SEC's 1975 proposal incited vociferous reactions from many interested partic . While the SEC claimed to have considered many of the outsiders' views in devising its final requirements, the provisions in ASR. No. 190 contained many of the deficiencies cited in the letters of comment. As a result, management felt that its opinions were largely ignored by the SEC.

In some circumstances the use of coercion by a policy setter may be quite appropriate. If persuasion and education strategies encouraging voluntary change are ineffective, as with ASR No. 151, the use of power may be necessary. The policy board may seek short-run behavioral compliance to secure an immediate remedial solution for an undesirable condition. The SEC apparently concluded that ignoring the impact of inflation on the corporation was a serious deficiency which could be at least partially overcome by the disclosure of replacement costs, and that the disadvantages of forced adoption of this innovation would be outweighed by the benefits to users. Finally, the SEC may have decided that actual experience with replacement-cost accounting would demonstrate its advantages, thus lessening long-run corporate resistance and facilitating eventual attitudinal acceptance.

While the SEC abandoned the use of an education strategy in favor of coercing the disclosure of replacement costs, it encouraged experimentation by firms in complying with the requirements. The provisions of ASR No. 190 permit flexibility in choosing from alternative approaches to implement the rule and formats to disclose the information. The intentional latitude for compliance was meant to encourage experimentation; however, this aspect of ASR No. 190 gave rise to major objections by corporate management. The lack of specific guidelines for implementation incited complaints regarding the imprecise nature of the disclosures, the heavy reliance on subjective judgments and assumptions, and the potentially misleading nature of the data. (See, for example, Carlson (1977) and DeWelt (1977).) While flexibility in developing disclosures may be advantageous to encouraging voluntary compliance in persuasive or educational programs, such latitude apparently enhanced the appearance of capriciousness by the SEC in devising the replacement cost disclosure requirements. The mandate of an experimental program intensifies the importance of a safe-harbor rule to protect the corporation from legal exposure.

THE PROMULGATION OF POLICY TO ENHANCE CHANGE

Prescriptions regarding appropriate strategies for policy setters to follow involve normative assertions which may be difficult to justify. However, past experience has indicated that certain approaches may be more functional for gaining acceptance of accounting innovations.

In the private sector

Resort to persuasion by a private-sector policy maker has largely been unsuccessful. Relying on euphuistic concepts such as good, correct, and reality, this approach ignores the critical political and sociological variables that vitally influence the acceptability of an innovation. On the other hand, the FASB does not have the power to mete out punishment and thus use coercion to gain compliance with its directives. While it does have strong indirect means to encourage cooperation (e.g., the withholding of an unqualified audit opinion on the firm's financial statements), direct punishment for deviant behavior can be mediated only when a more powerful body sanctions the FASB's directives. Additionally, attempts to use authority which extend beyond the FASB's power base may undermine its credibility and eventually result in less cooperation by the business community.

Greater chances for success in changing management's accounting practices appear to come from the use of education strategies. By giving full recognition to the norms of the business community and to the potential conflict of an innovation with those values, the policy setter can embark on experimental and informational programs to demonstrate the use of the new practice and influence management's values and predispositions. This approach also encourages two-way communication so that various aspects of the proposed change can be altered to make it more acceptable to management.

In the public sector

Possession of a significant amount of power by the SEC precludes the direct use of persuasion on the business community, since the mention of a preferred accounting alternative presents the potential for sanctions for deviant behavior. Both education and coercion have been used in the past, at times in consort. The SEC may use education alone by issuing a directive in which a certain change is suggested or urged. The business community would do well to heed such suggestions, since at least a modicum of experimentation might forestall mandated compliance. For example, if more firms had disclosed inventory profits pursuant to ASR No. 151, the SEC might have been convinced that efforts at improved reporting under inflationary conditions were being made and forced change (i.e., ASR No. 190) was unnecessary. The SEC can effectively use education and experimentation if it wishes to gradually encourage the business community to change and to maximize the possibility that such change will be accepted.

In those situations where coercion appears appropriate, the central question becomes whether a period of education, experimentation, research, and communication would lessen the adverse effects of a coercive change. The two years of cooperative interplay between the

SEC and business community preceding the requirement for line-of-business reporting demonstrate that coupling education with coercion can reduce corporate resistance, foster the recognition of benefits, and encourage attitudinal acceptance. Insufficient communication and experimentation prior to the mandate for replacement cost accounting contributed to the widespread negative reaction by management to ASR No. 190, and the concomitant resentment toward the SEC.

In formulating its recommendations regarding the disclosure of soft information, the SEC Advisory Committee on Corporate Disclosure (1977, pp. 344-347, 354-355) considered the SEC's role as a change agent and the use of education to foster voluntary experimentation. Four advantages were cited to the use of a voluntary approach rather than coercion: (1) the SEC does not currently have a basis for establishing the specific rules and regulations necessary for mandatory implementation of these disclosures, (2) all public companies should not be required to bear the expenses and other complications associated with these disclosures, (3) public companies should not be forced to endure the potential risks of liability for inaccurate forecasts, and (4) due to a lack of operating history, or because of general economic and industry conditions, many companies would find compliance extremely difficult.

Note that the first and fourth reasons relate to the operational problems encountered by corporations in implementing new disclosure requirements. Such considerations were largely ignored in the SEC's mandate for replacement costs, and management was thus forced to undertake programs of nonvoluntary experimentation. The second and third reasons give recognition to problems that may foster managerial resistance to a change; corporations with high expected costs or fearful of legal liability might be expected to object to the proposal and thus be less inclined to voluntarily change.

The Advisory Committee explicitly considered lack of cooperation by corporations as the major disadvantage to reliance upon education and experimentation. Yet it concluded that management has strong incentives to disclose more than the minimum information required.

> One drawback to a voluntary system is that many issuers may choose not to provide any information. . . . If the information is truly valuable to investment decision-makers, then market forces, i.e., demand by investors, may be a strong force to impel such disclosures. There are indications that good disclosure practices have positive effects (Advisory Committee on Corporate Disclosure 1977, p. 355).

These market forces center on the proclivity of financial analysts to follow more closely those corporations with full disclosure, and the importance of interest in the corporation by the financial-analyst community to the liquidity and price of the firm's securities. This has a cumulative effect, since changes in reporting practices by one company place competitive pressure on other firms to follow.

For both the FASB and SEC, then, the use of an education strategy appears highly desirable for gaining acceptance of change by the business community. For the FASB, this strategy is almost necessary. For the SEC, education is also functional when the decision to use coercion has been made. The use of education may involve additional efforts by policy setters, result in higher costs, and delay the implementation of an innovation. However, the enhanced likelihood that the change will be accepted and implemented without dysfunctional consequences such as resistance, resentment, loss of credibility, or attempts at circumvention appear to outweigh the disadvantages. A trial period is also more equitable to the business community which has high stakes in financial reporting practices. Using education and experimentation does not mean corporate management is assuming a dominant role in establishing standards. Instead, adequate consideration is being given to its views, the impact of changes on its status quo, and the stability of existing norms.

SUMMARY

Three general types of change strategy predominate for securing acceptance of innovations: persuasion, education, and coercion. Both the private and public sectors have used various strategies in attempting to gain compliance with policy directives. Probably most influential in the strategy employed has been the type of power possessed by the policy setter.

With a very weak power position, the APB relied on persuading managers and accountants that its standards were normatively correct, as attempted in the investment tax credit and pooling of interests issues. It soon learned that sole reliance on persuasion was unworkable, and it retreated to addressing uncontroversial areas where inducement was easier or unnecessary. The FASB began employing education strategies, fostering greater attention to the business community's interests, as with the formulation of recommendations for inflation accounting. The private sector is largely precluded from using coercion, unless backed by an agency with enforcement powers.

Because the SEC possesses a great deal of power, its directives are more compelling than persuasive. If the SEC wishes solely to use persuasion, it must do so through a private-sector policy board. Education strategies have been used beginning with line-of-business reporting, and have resulted in greater understanding of a final policy statement. Coercion has been the predominant strategy, best exemplified by the replacement cost disclosure requirement.

Presently the FASB still relies largely on persuasion, while the SEC most frequently uses coercion. Both groups of policy setters might enhance the acceptability of their decisions by greater use of education strategies. By stressing experimentation and information, management's norms and opinions are more adequately considered and acceptance of directives is encouraged.

Chapter Six

FACTORS INFLUENCING MANAGEMENT'S REACTION TO ACCOUNTING STANDARDS

Acceptance or rejection by corporate management of a proposed change in accounting practices is a complex decision, affected by a myriad of interacting factors. This chapter considers four categories of forces found to influence the decision: (1) resistance to change inherent within the individual and social system, (2) aspects specific to the innovation, (3) communication channels used to diffuse the proposed change, and (4) social system effects.

GENERAL FORCES RESISTING CHANGE

Influences fostering resistance to change in general exist in both the individual and the social system (Watson 1966). Within an individual, established attitudes, dependence on others, and insecurity give rise to forces such as homeostasis, habit, primacy, selective perception, and retention which act to inhibit movement toward change. Corresponding inhibitors exist within social systems: conformity to norms, cultural coherence and interrelationships, vested interests, and distrust of those outside the social unit. A successful program of planned social change focuses on reducing these forces of resistance through careful consideration of the characteristics of the innovation, the nature of the target social system, the role of the policy maker, and appropriate communication channels.

The natural resistance to change may prevent acceptance of radical innovations unless corporate opposition is low or coercion is used. It may also inhibit attempts to correct deficient financial reporting practices. This is exemplified by comments received during the

FASB's post-enactment review of FAS No. 8 on foreign currency translation:

> Despite the criticism of FASB-8 at the Stamford gathering, many executives share the admonition that DuPont's [Comptroller C. Raeford] Minix gave the board, warning it to proceed carefully. "Wholesale changes may prove more upsetting than the status quo," he says ("A Major Audit for FASB-8" 1978).

Resistance by management has been cited as only partially responsible for the lack of innovation in accounting (Sterling 1973). Also important is the separation of research from education and practice. Accounting educators often teach only those methods that are used in practice. In their roles as managers and practicing accountants, students utilize these methods and oppose new practices as modifications in the status quo. When combined with corporate resistance to changes which threaten vested interests, the inhibition to innovation within the system itself is quite high. To reduce the inherent forces thwarting change, accounting education might be broadened to include exposure to research findings which represent more "desirable" practices.

ASPECTS SPECIFIC TO THE INNOVATION

Intrinsic elements of an innovation are those attributes which are inherent in the specific change and thus independent of the diffusion process. Since they influence management's innovation decision, policy makers should be cognizant of these factors and incorporate them in any plan for change. The three most salient intrinsic elements that have been noted in innovation theory are the innovation's form (directly observable physical appearance and substance), function (impact on the change target's customary existence), and meaning (perception of the innovation by the target). These intrinsic elements have facilitated the identification of five characteristics of an innovation which influence its acceptability by management.

The importance of perceptions

Before discussing the five characteristics, it should be emphasized that the meaning or perception of an innovation is a critical factor in gaining acceptance of financial reporting practices. Since perceptions are individualistic and highly subjective, the meaning that management ascribes to a proposed change may differ from that which the policy maker wishes to impart. Anticipation of these perceptions should be part of the ex ante consideration of potential consequences, and successful assessment of the business community's existing norms and values will yield more accurate anticipation of the meaning which the innovation will have to management.

The importance of perceptions in gauging reactions to proposed changes in accounting was the focus of a study into the semantic aspects of accounting constructs, and the impact of connotative meaning on gaining acceptance of new ideas for internal reporting by accountants and managers (Flamholtz and Cook 1978). The subjects of the study were found to distinguish between traditional and nontraditional practices, the latter including concepts such as human resource accounting, social accounting, and accounting for intangibles. This finding was attributed to a "semantic halo effect" in which generalizations regarding the attributes of an idea are formulated based on its degree of perceived novelty.

> The existence of this semantic halo effect does *not* necessarily mean that there actually are significant differences in the operationalizability [the distinguishing factor] of new accounting constructs; rather, it means that the nontraditional constructs are perceived in that way (Flamholtz and Cook 1978, p. 135).

Thus accounting for intangibles was grouped with human resource accounting by the subjects, even though the former concept is not a new idea. The implication for engineering change in accounting is that reactions to innovations will depend on the perceptions of the proposed change's compatibility with customary reporting practices, and such perceptions may be subject to a semantic halo effect.

The importance of meaning for gaining adoption of innovations was also studied by focusing on the differences in perceptions among various accounting interest groups (Hicks 1978). The objective of this research was to identify similarities and differences in perceptions by various social units, potentially an important factor for identifying barriers to the acceptance of innovations and for predicting the success of a program of planned change. (The results and implications of this study will be more fully discussed in the subsequent section on Social System Effects.)

Given the closeness of the FASB and the SEC to the business community, it is doubtful that they are unaware of management's value scheme for financial reporting. For example, policy makers should anticipate strong negative reactions to disclosure requirements perceived as yielding subjective measurements, detrimental to management's performance record, reducing flexibility in reporting practices, or costly to implement. Rather than being ignorant of corporate opposition to replacement cost accounting, it is more likely that the SEC chose to ignore management's perceptions of the innovation. Functional programs of planned change involve not only awareness of change target perceptions, but also incorporation of those beliefs into the plan.

Five characteristics of an innovation that involve these intrinsic elements have been recognized as influencing an innovation adoption decision: (1) relative advantage, (2) compatibility with norms, (3) complexity in use, (4) trialability of the change, and (5) observability of perceived benefits (Rogers and Shoemaker 1971, pp. 135-137). As these characteristics are discussed, it should be kept in mind that what is important is the *perception* of the attributes, since these cognitions will determine the innovation's acceptability.

Relative advantage

Primary among the characteristics is the relative advantage of the change, or the benefits which management believes will accrue from adopting the innovation. Such advantages are often measured in economic terms and may include expectations of economic profitability, implementation costs, attendant risks, time savings, immediacy of the benefits, and the like. These costs are easily misestimated, since biases exist on the part of those who are assessing the relative advantages and thus concerned with avoiding uncertainty and forestalling involvement in the firm's activities by outside parties.

One aspect affecting the relative advantage of an innovation is the existence of a crisis. This situation undermines the status quo and enhances any benefits that the change might seem to offer. An example is the Brazilian accounting system which underwent radical changes as the result of an economic crisis. Extensive and high rates of inflation in Brazil severely impaired the adequacy of historical cost accounting. In the 1960s, a system of inflation accounting, whereby all transactions and accounts are adjusted with a price-level index, became widely used and accepted. Inflation accounting is now the norm, and movements back to the historical cost basis for financial transactions and reporting would be perceived as disadvantageous and met with strong resistance.

The importance of the relative advantage of a proposed accounting standard in policy setting has been previously recognized by policy makers. Since accounting standards affect the economic welfare of various parties, it is natural to expect these parties to attempt to improve their statuses by influencing the changes which policy boards endorse. Following his term as Chairman of the FASB, Armstrong (1977) admitted that the business community could be expected to respond to a proposed standard when it perceived an impact on its economic well-being might result. Armstrong continued, however, to naively implore corporate managers to subordinate their self-interest to the "public good" when formulating their positions on policies.

Information inductance as previously discussed is a vital aspect of the relative advantage of an innovation. In assessing a change in financial reporting practices and its impact on managerial performance reports, the information sender will consider feedback effects from the use of the disclosures by outsiders. Such use may include evaluation of management's accomplishments, regulation of corporate operations, modification of alternatives open to the entity, and establishment of a position vis-à-vis the firm as in labor negotiations, supply pricing, and competitor reactions. These feedback effects represent the advantages and disadvantages to management that are associated with the proposed change.

Recently, a positive theory of standard setting has been suggested, in which management's position on proposed accounting standards is determined by the perceived impact of the change on the manager's personal well-being (Watts and Zimmerman 1978). Management's goal of maximizing its own wealth can be accomplished in two ways: (1) An increase in the firm's cash flows which raises share prices, thereby increasing the value of stock and stock options. Cash flow can be enhanced through lower taxes, higher regulatory rates, lower political costs (as from antitrust proceedings), and lower information production costs. (2) An increase in management incentive compensation which, however, reduces the firm's cash flow and suppresses stock prices.

Management's position on a proposed standard can be predicted by assessing the potential impact on the firm's earnings. If a change in financial reporting is expected to raise corporate profits, the firm's directors may make downward adjustments in management's compensation plans. This offers little incentive for management to support an accounting standard which enhances earnings. On the other hand, a proposed change which lowers reported profits may increase management's wealth via the positive impact on cash flows and stock prices from tax, regulatory, and political factors.

For large firms that are regulated or subject to political pressure, the following is hypothesized:

> ... we predict that managers have greater incentives to choose accounting standards which report lower earnings (thereby increasing cashflows, firm value, and their welfare) due to tax, political, and regulatory considerations than to choose accounting standards which report higher earnings and, thereby, increase their incentive compensation (Watts and Zimmerman 1978, p. 118).

For small unregulated corporations, management's analysis would focus on changes in incentive compensation and tax effects. In all cases, the impact on information production costs would be considered.

This theoretical framework was empirically tested by examining corporate positions submitted to the FASB on the discussion memorandum proposing general price-level adjusted (GPLA) financial statements. All those firms which would report increases in income from adoption of the innovation registered opposition to the change. Large corporations whose earnings would be decreased supported the proposal, while small firms with potentially lower earnings were opposed.

> This suggests that reduced political and/or tax costs outweigh information production and/or management compensation factors in determining management's position on GPLA only for very large firms. For most other firms, information production costs dominate (Watts and Zimmerman 1978, p. 126).

The cutoff defining a large firm was a rank of between 18 and 22 on the Fortune 500.

An important implication of this finding is that the relevant social system in a change situation may need to be defined more closely than just the business community. To appropriately assess the impact of relative advantages on management's reaction, it may be necessary to consider separately large and small firms, keeping in mind that the cutoff for "large" is determined by the probability of government interference. As more and more firms come under political scrutiny and/or are subject to regulation, increasing support for standards that decrease reported earnings may be expected.

Corporate reaction to segment reporting as proposed by the Federal Trade Commission in the late 1960s illustrates the importance of regulation to the perception of relative advantage. Segment information was sought by government agencies to monitor the intensifying merger movement. The business community uniformly opposed this disclosure requirement, fearing its merger activities would be curtailed through increased antitrust and divestiture actions.

The split in corporate reaction to successful-efforts oil and gas accounting, as originally required under FAS No. 19, demonstrates the impact of firm size. This accounting standard did not represent a change to most large oil companies that currently use successful-efforts accounting. The small independent oil and gas producers, however, use full costing and thus capitalize development and exploration costs. Compliance with FAS No. 19 would have reduced earnings, with alleged detrimental effects on stock prices and the ability to raise capital. Such contentions are inconsistent with the efficient market hypothesis. Investors can readily determine the impact on a firm's earnings of full-cost versus successful-efforts accounting; thus no new information would have been provided under FAS No. 19. Additionally, this standard would affect the cash flows of the firm only if there was a tax effect from a change in accounting method. (A recent study (Mayer-Sommer 1979) has found low levels of understanding and acceptance by controllers of the efficient market theory and research findings.)

The arguments presented by opponents to FAS No. 19 demonstrate the importance of *perceived* relative advantages. Opposition from the management of independents might have arisen because increases in the value of stock and stock options were not expected to offset decreased incentive compensation. If the new standard had represented a change to the major oil and gas producers, support from that group might have been forthcoming. Although FAS No. 19 would have reduced their reported earnings, cash flows might have been enhanced from lower taxes and reduced government intervention (e.g., jawboning to keep prices down). The expected increase in personal wealth held in the form of stock compensation would exceed the reduction in incentive compensation, thus motivating management to support the change.

The low perception of relative advantages from disclosing replacement costs was largely responsible for corporate opposition to ASR No. 190. The time, effort, and out-of-pocket costs of compliance were expected to be excessive. Implementation difficulties due to the lack of operational guidelines were purported to yield subjective and unverifiable data, amenable to manipulation and bias. Corporate management was reluctant to assume the risks of legal liability for such unreliable disclosures. Because of the crucial role of assumptions, judgments, and estimations, claims were made that the data would be inconsistent, noncomparable, nonunderstandable, deceptive, unrealistic, incomplete and, as a result, totally useless to financial statement readers.

More concern was evidenced, however, over how investors would use the disclosures. It was feared that the firm's net income would be adjusted downward to incorporate the negative impact from the higher replacement cost of sales and depreciation, with no upward revisions to incorporate operating cost savings or gains and losses on monetary items. Anxiety was expressed over the impact that naive use of such disclosures might have on the economy's equity markets. The SEC may have actually enhanced the perception of low benefits to complying registrants in ASR No. 190 by cautioning against "simplistic use" of the data presented, stating there are substantial theoretical problems in determining an income effect, encouraging investors not to revise net income, stressing the data are not comparable among companies, and noting that the amounts are subject to errors of estimation.

In general, reactions to the various proposals for inflation accounting can be attributed to industry- and firm-specific factors. General price-level adjusted financial statements are favored by many corporations which are characteristically highly leveraged. Replacement cost accounting is especially opposed by firms in capital-intensive industries. Companies with nonmarketable assets disapprove of alternatives based on current selling prices.

> Though the protracted arguments about the relative merits of these and other rival systems have not generally overtly recognized the vested interests that stand to gain or lose by the way the argument goes, the political implications of inflation accounting have probably had as much respon-

sibility for the difficulty in reaching agreement on the direction in which to move as have the technical problems involved (Solomons 1978a, p. 69).

It was significant that the FASB's exposure draft for inflation accounting is founded on flexibility and allowed corporations to choose between constant-dollar or current-cost accounting, depending on which was deemed most appropriate. If the final standard had retained this flexibility, the perception of disadvantages by the business community might have been lessened, and the acceptability of the FASB's proposal enhanced.

The impact of increased accounting costs from new disclosure requirements has also become central in assessing the relative advantage of recent changes. Anticipation of high compliance costs was a major factor cited by many of the firms which vehemently opposed replacement cost accounting as required under ASR No. 190. These costs include not only expenses incurred to engage outsiders such as accountants and appraisers to assist in the calculations, but also the opportunity costs from diverting corporate personnel into increased accounting tasks.

Once accounting policy makers relinquish the notion that they are seeking "correct" accounting practices, and admit they are operating in a political arena where the sociological aspects of their decisions must be considered, the positions of the various affected parties will have to be given full recognition. The perceptions of relative advantage and the schism between large and small firms on changes which reduce reported earnings are concrete examples of the forces a policy setter will encounter. At this point it must be recognized that a final policy decision involves a social value judgment wherein one group benefits to the detriment of someone else. However, the issue is clouded since both perceived and real impacts will be operative.

Compatibility with norms

The second important characteristic influencing adoption of an innovation is compatibility, or the perceived consistency of a proposed change with management's values, norms, past experiences, attitudes, and needs. This variable inextricably involves the sociological and cultural attributes of the business community. The greater the congruence with existing norms, the less change the innovation represents.

While compatibility relates to a specific change, the social system's general attitude toward innovating is an important sociological variable. Prior experiences with innovations which have failed may create a negative attitude on the part of management toward the policy setter. For example, frustrations in complying with ASR No. 190 may significantly diminish voluntary disclosure of other "soft" information such as the forward-looking projections encouraged by the SEC. Compatibility may be enhanced, however, by associating the innovation with other changes which are more palatable.

The value scheme of the business community must be clearly distinguished from that of the accounting profession. The latter group is concerned with financial reporting standards which are user oriented, stressing information useful to investors for decision making. Management, on the other hand, adopts a user perspective only to the extent necessary for maintaining its equity market. Less importance is accordingly placed on qualities such as relevance, timeliness, lack of bias, consistency, uniformity, and comparability. The business community is more concerned with legal liability for the adequacy and accuracy of its financial disclosures. It thus stresses values such as objectivity, reliability, accuracy, verifiability, and conservatism. Again, however, it is the perception that these attributes are possessed by a proposed standard which determines management's stance toward the change.

Occasionally it may be difficult to distinguish relative advantages from compatibility. Corporate reaction to FAS No. 2, which requires current expensing of all research and development costs, demonstrates the separate operation of these factors. While opposition was voiced to the negative impact on reported earnings which results, expensing all costs as incurred is highly compatible with corporate norms since it is an objective, conservative approach to accounting for costs with uncertain future benefits.

Proposals for the disclosure of forecasts exemplify the problems with gaining acceptance of innovations which are incongruous with the change target's norms. Projections are primarily made for the benefit of financial statement users, and the advantages to a corporation of publishing such disclosures are not clear. The information has little relevance to assessing management's past operating performance. And while disclosure of an optimistic forecast might seem to encourage investment in the firm's stock, subsequent failure to attain those goals could have detrimental consequences. More germane to management's position on forecasting is the lack of compatibility with financial reporting customs. Projections of future performance involve many subjective evaluations and critically depend on the adequacy of assumptions underlying the data. As a result, the disclosures are not verifiable and may be inaccurate and unreliable. This situation enhances management's fear of legal liability for imprecise data and of potential responsibility for future results which fall short of projections.

Evidence of these attitudes was found in two studies conducted just after the SEC lifted its ban on the publication of earnings forecasts in 1973 (Asebrook and Carmichael 1973; Carpenter and Daily 1974). The two separate surveys polled members of the FEI and controllers of Fortune 500 corporations. Overwhelming opposition was cited to being required, or even encouraged, to publish forecasted income statements. Respondents claimed that the average investor would misunderstand or misinterpret such projections. In a study subsequent to the 1975 SEC proposal, over 90 percent of the 375 chief financial officers replying stated they would cease issuing projections to all outsiders if they were required to file the disclosures with the SEC (Foster 1978, pp. 538–539). The SEC's 1976 and 1978 forecasting proposals gave fuller recognition to management's financial reporting norms by permitting rather than requiring the disclosure of projections, and by stressing experimentation and flexibility. The 1978 guidelines may receive wider acceptance by the business community than did the 1976 proposal, since the former provides for protection from legal liability through a safe-harbor rule.

Complexity in use

The complexity factor is the perceived difficulty in understanding and implementing the innovation. The dual dimension is important: both comprehension and calculation influence the perception of complexity. This aspect will be determined by the change target's existing technical skills, knowledge, education, prior experiences, availability of outside consultants, expected learning curve, and the like. Anticipated costs of implementation are not directly involved, as they influence the perceived relative advantage.

Complexity may involve factors outside the innovation itself, as was found in a study on the connotative meaning of various accounting concepts (Flamholtz and Cook 1978). For the use of accounting innovations in internal reports, the factor that distinguished management's attitude toward traditional versus nontraditional concepts was evaluative/operationalization. Contrary to familiar accounting constructs, nontraditional ideas were perceived as arduous to operationalize when viewed in terms of complexity, completeness, and measurability. A semantic halo effect was posited, whereby managers generalize that all nontraditional accounting concepts are difficult to operationalize, regardless of the actual difficulty with implementing and understanding the change.

The importance of attending to operational aspects for successfully gaining adoption of a change has been aptly recognized by accounting policy makers. In 1969, the AICPA began issuing interpretations intended to assist in the application of standards to specific situations. The FASB has continued this practice by promulgating interpretations of its directives, while the SEC issues SABs for this purpose.

Perhaps the classic example of a highly complex accounting standard is APB Opinion No. 15, which stipulates procedures for the computation and disclosure of earnings per share. This standard contains detailed rules for performing two earnings per share calculations, using both historical and pro forma or predictive information. Incorporation of the potential impact of conversions, options, warrants, and the like is accomplished through arbitrary rules and assumptions. Allegations that many potential situations are treated in seemingly inconsistent and illogical ways has fostered contentions that the directive is difficult for management to implement and the resulting computations have dubious meaning.

A more contemporary illustration is offered by lease accounting as governed under FAS No. 13. Following the promulgation of this standard, articles began appearing in the professional literature attempting to interpret the requirements both operationally and conceptually. Because the rules are so complex, many uncertainties and contradictions remain. Since the lease standard was issued in 1976, several amendments and interpretations have resulted. Corporate managers not only have difficulty in applying the rules, they also lose sight of the meaning of a capitalized lease. Such a complex environment endangers acceptance of the standard by management.

In designing its replacement cost disclosure requirements, the SEC appeared to be cognizant of implementation difficulties. Six SABs were issued prior to the compliance deadline discussing possible definitions, computational techniques, and disclosures. An advisory committee was created to guide corporate compliance and resolve specific problems. As discussed previously, major objections arose to ASR No. 190 for the SEC's failure to issue specific guidelines for determining replacement costs. Indeed, the SEC may have enhanced management's perception of complexity by stating in ASR No. 190 that the disclosures cannot be calculated with precision, numerous assumptions which vary over time and among companies must be made, measurement techniques are not fully developed or standardized, and difficult conceptual and empirical judgments are necessary. By focusing on these implementation deficiencies, the SEC may have thwarted the adoption process.

Trialability of the change

A fourth characteristic is trialability or divisibility, defined as the extent to which an innovation can be implemented on a partial basis. This factor may involve limited adoption of a change by each firm, or complete implementation but by only part of the change target social system. Selective implementation may be seen as advantageous if management perceives lower risks from partial adoption, and thus is encouraged to experiment. Dysfunctional consequences may obtain, however, if the limited implementation yields fragmented, complex, and noncomparable disclosures. Such results are most likely if the innovation is not entirely suited to divisibility.

The importance of the trialability factor was recognized by former APB staff member Dale Gerboth (1972) in his suggestions for an incremental approach to policy making (The application of incrementalism to policy making was done in most depth by Charles E. Lindblom as cited by Gerboth (1972, p. 48n).) Following this method, relatively small deviations from the status quo are the foundation for proposed policy changes. And rather than relying on a priori analyses to identify needed changes, policies are adopted based on feedback from affected parties regarding prior innovations. The incremental approach relies on one basic tenet: the smaller the magnitude of the change, the greater the chance of acceptance. This viewpoint was adopted by the APB in its later years.

The gradual inculcation of change is a characteristic of ASR No. 253, the SEC's directive for oil and gas accounting (Cooper, Flory, and Grossman 1979). This ruling provides for the development over a three-year period of reserve recognition accounting, a current value approach for oil and gas reserves. Provisions have been made for the interim period to enhance the transition to reserve recognition accounting, aid in the development and implementation of accounting techniques, and test for feasibility. First-year requirements include supplementary disclosures of historical financial and operating information, including the quantities of proved oil and gas reserves and cash flow from production activities. For the second year of compliance, a supplementary earnings summary with income according to reserve recognition accounting is to be prepared. Finally, in the third year, reserve recognition accounting is to be adopted in the primary financial statements.

In settling on the final requirements for replacement cost disclosures, the SEC utilized the divisibility of the innovation. Recognition of gains and losses on monetary items was not required, the disclosures were not integrated into the traditional financial statements, the data could be unaudited, and calculation of operating cost savings was encouraged but not mandated. Ironically, some of these provisions led management and others to criticize ASR No. 190 because it provided for "partial" disclosure of the impact of inflation on the firm's financial condition. But this partial nature was intentional, as the SEC sought to encourage experimentation. Resistance to the innovation would undoubtedly have been intensified with more radical departures from the traditional historical-cost model.

Trialability of an innovation can also be enhanced with voluntary experimental programs for change. The AICPA encouraged partial adoption of inflation-adjusted statements, but its program called for complete implementation by firms willing to voluntarily experiment with four models: general price-level statements, historical cost statements with LIFO inventory and current cost depreciation, financial statements with part historical cost and part current cost amounts, and current value statements (AICPA 1977). Experiences regarding the concepts and measurements, meaningfulness of the results, and problems and costs of implementation were also solicited.

The FASB (1978e) also focused on trialability in formulating its 1978 proposal for accounting for changing prices. Flexibility and experimentation were purposely encouraged, as through the choice between constant-dollar or current-cost accounting, to foster the development of techniques for reporting the impact of inflation. Even in its final requirements where both methods are mandated, the FASB views this as a learning process, enhancing the development of new approaches as deemed appropriate in the corporation's specific circumstances.

Observability of perceived benefits

Finally, observability, or the degree to which the results from adopting a change are visible and can be communicated to management, is a characteristic of the innovation. Focusing on the positive aspects, the clear existence of net benefits enhances the innovation's acceptability. Social system effects are involved, as communication among members of the business community will influence the visibility of expected advantages.

The observability factor has been studied to determine why management is reluctant to disclose more information in annual reports to stockholders. An information value hypothesis was tested:

> ... management is reluctant to disclose additional information items in corporate reports because it does not share the objectives and perceptions of investors and, consequently, assigns lower information values to those items than investors do (Chandra and Greenball 1977, p. 144).

Low observability of benefits from expanded disclosures was thus posited.

In a questionnaire sent to financial executives and security analysts, respondents were asked to value the importance of each of fifty-eight information items. In general, when compared with security analysts, financial executives placed lower values on controversial disclosures (e.g., price-level adjusted statements, purchase versus pooling), but higher values on basic and commonly disclosed information items. The information value hypothesis was supported, and the discrepancy between management's and investors' use of financial disclosures was cited as explanation for corporate resistance to demands for more information. The observability factor was thus identified, evidence was found for its existence, and it was demonstrated to be a critical element in gaining acceptance of change.

The observability of perceived benefits can be enhanced through the proper use of strategy. Programs of persuasion can heighten the visibility of advantages to the change target. Education strategies which involve experimentation may reduce initial resistance by encouraging management to experiment with new methods. First-hand experience with the innovation and its advantages is the ultimate means for gaining observability. Innovations which lend themselves to divisibility or trialability are especially amenable to demonstrating visibility through education. An example of the successful use of education to demonstrate benefits and lessen initial resistance is the two years of research allowed by the SEC prior to adopting rules for segment reporting. When finally implemented, corporations viewed the disclosures as enhancing their competitive position in the equity markets and little opposition was encountered.

COMMUNICATION ASPECTS

Apart from characteristics specific to the innovation, the channels used to communicate new ideas can influence their acceptance. The use of normal communication channels, such as FASs and ASRs, enhances compatibility with management's norms, as promulgation of the directive then occurs in the expected manner. Deviations outside the normal communication system may create uncertainty apart from that caused by the proposed change. The FASB's (1978d) initiation of FACs represents the introduction of a new communication mechanism into the accounting environment. Before stating its conclusions, the FASB used two pages to explain the purpose, scope, authority, and weight of FACs, focusing on the differences from FASs. Lacking in precedent, these pronouncements are entirely new to management and accountants. The FASB may accordingly experience low acceptance of its proposal, predominantly caused by uncertainty regarding the communication medium rather than disagreement with the ideas.

A second aspect of the communication factor is the clarity with which the requirements are stated. Confusing and ambiguous messages can thwart acceptance of the change irrespective of the innovation's characteristics. While this can heighten the perceived complexity of the new practice, communication regarding the idea itself can create or mitigate uncertainty. By including examples of application in the appendices to a FAS, the FASB attempts to clearly communicate how a new procedure is to be implemented. In contrast, the SEC often neglects this aspect. A frequent criticism of ASR No. 190 was the use of ambiguous terms and lack of explicit guidelines, resulting in uncertainty regarding implementation and fostering incomparable disclosures among firms ("Replacement Costs: Clarification or Confusion?" 1976; Carlson 1977). Although contrary to its intention of encouraging experimentation, if the SEC had more definitively stated its expectations, confusion over implementation might have been lessened.

SOCIAL SYSTEM EFFECTS IN THE ACCOUNTING ENVIRONMENT

The innovation plan should include a study of the power structure of the social system. A power elite may exist which in essence makes the innovation decision. Less influential are opinion leaders to whom the social system members look for advice and approval of proposed changes. These two groups are crucial to achieving adoption, and the policy maker should focus on compatibility of the innovation with the value scheme of the power elite or opinion leaders. Also important is obtaining grass root or peer approval, as once a new standard gains popularity it may spread through this support. Resistance, however, can also be inculcated in this fashion.

Two groups of opinion leaders can be identified as important to accounting policy setters. First is the management of the firms which are considered industry leaders, as the reactions and opinions of such individuals are highly influential within the business community and their respective industries. Special interest groups from the insurance, banking, and petroleum industries have become actively involved in the formulation of specific standards. Industry committees were created to deal with the problems of complying with ASR No. 190. Gaining support from the opinion leaders of such groups would have facilitated the adoption process. Second is the public accounting profession, as corporate management often looks to its CPAs for interpretation of a proposed standard, assessment of the impact on the firm, and appropriate response. Had the SEC concentrated on gaining the acceptance of replacement costs by the accounting profession before issuing ASR No. 190, corporate resistance might have been lessened.

A study of the importance of social system effects in gaining acceptance of change in accounting focused on four interest groups: academicians, investment analysts, CPAs, and financial executives. The perceptions of these groups regarding various innovations were sought to determine the acceptance of the changes. The importance of this factor was stated as follows:

> ... differences in perception may provide evidence which could help predict barriers to the change process. Furthermore, evidence of similarities of perceptions as to innovations could indicate that adoption of an innovation is highly probable or highly improbable due to the consensus of perceptions (Hicks 1978, pp. 372-373).

Such perceptions are also important to changes which have been mandated, as these cognitions will influence the stance of acceptance or resistance taken toward coerced implementation of the innovation.

Identification of differences between interest groups regarding the perceived need for a change would indicate the existence of "system effects." These social system influences will affect the acceptance of a change and may cause conflict between groups if the perceived needs differ. Thus not only is the individual's felt need for a change important, but the relation of that motivation to the perceptions of other social system groups will affect the change process.

To study the potential differences in perceptions, a total of 480 questionnaires were mailed to members of the four accounting interest groups. Responses were received from 265 participants. For each of thirty innovations, respondents were asked to rate (1) the perceived need for adoption of the innovation, and (2) the perceived extent of adoption by the end of 1975 and 1995 (used to measure rate of adoption). For twenty-six of the thirty innovations, significant differences were found in the perceptions by the four groups of a need for adoption of the innovation. Additionally, for fourteen of the innovations, there were significant differences in the perceived rate of adoption of the innovations. The finding of a relationship between the perception of an innovation and membership in an interest group led to the conclusion that system effects were operative in the innovation decision process.

Further analysis revealed that, in general, academicians had a high need for inculcating change, while CPAs and financial executives were more resistant to adopting innovations. The following observation was made:

> If the current authoritative bodies assume a more active role in the future, as to promoting change in the accounting profession, they are likely to have the support of academia. However, substantial resistance to change could be expected from CPAs and financial executives. Therefore, the potential for conflict as innovations are implemented is substantial (Hicks 1978, p. 386).

This reinforces the importance of identifying all relevant parties in the social system, including the power elite and opinion leaders, determining the extent of their influence, and ascertaining their position on proposed changes.

To enhance future adoption of innovations, research is needed into causes for a low perception of need for change by the resistant interest groups. Such research might find that characteristics of the innovation, such as incompatibility with norms or complexity in implementation, are primary forces impeding adoption. A complete study would also include identifying factors of the change environment which are present when a high need for adoption is expressed, as perhaps high relative advantage or unambiguous communication.

SUMMARY

To study the sociological aspects of management's role in the formulation of accounting policy, the factors influencing reactions to proposed accounting changes were identified. Four categories of forces dominate the business community's stance of support or opposition to an accounting standard. First are the general forces resisting change inherent within the individual and the social system. Aspects specific to the innovation, or the characteristics of the proposed change, comprise the second category of influencing factors. It is management's perception of these characteristics that is most critical in reactions to a specific innovation. Five types of characteristics determine the intrinsic nature of the proposed change: (1) the relative advantages from adopting the innovation, (2) compatibility of the new practice with norms and experiences, (3) complexity in understanding and implementing the requirement, (4) trialability or the extent to which the change can be partially implemented, and (5) observability or the degree to which consequences from adopting the innovation are foreseeable.

The third category of forces involves the communication channels used to impart proposals and requirements. Uncertainty arising from the method of communication can impede diffusion of the innovation. Finally, social system effects of the accounting environment comprise the fourth category. This factor encompasses the power elite and opinion leaders who critically influence acceptance of the standard by the corporate community.

Appendix

PREVIOUS RESEARCH ON MANAGEMENT'S ADOPTION OF ACCOUNTING CHANGES

Prior theories and empirical research have focused on responses from the business community to changes in financial reporting practices. The purpose of this appendix is to consider alternative explanations of management's role in the disclosure system, and to compare research findings related to the various theories. The studies that have concentrated on the characteristics of accounting innovations which influence management's adoption decision are described first. Theories and research not focusing on accounting changes as innovations are contained in the second section.

CHARACTERISTICS OF ACCOUNTING STANDARDS AS INNOVATIONS

In the 1970s researchers began observing the adoption of new reporting practices by the business community. Management's actions regarding accounting policies could not be totally explained by economic forces. Emphasis thus shifted to identifying the factors which influence management's decision. Six studies have focused on the characteristics of accounting changes which determine reactions to innovations.

Accounting changes for tax benefits

Charles Tritschler (1970) studied whether French corporations revalued their assets for tax purposes during the interval from 1946 to 1959. Given that tax benefits from lower reported earnings exceeded compliance costs, Tritschler expected firms to make price-level adjustments. Analysis revealed that by 1960, 12 percent of the eligible firms had adopted revaluation, representing approximately 60 percent of the economy's fixed assets. Tritschler concluded that this "irrational" failure to minimize taxes by more corporations must be attributable to a characteristic of the innovation like complexity of implementation, and that adoption of an innovation is not solely based on the desire to maximize profits.

This finding is consistent with the positive theory discussed in the previous section on Relative Advantage. This theory suggests that large firms will support changes which reduce reported net income in order to enhance cash flows and stock prices. Thus while only 12 percent of the French firms revalued assets, they must have represented the largest corporations since they accounted for a majority of the economy's fixed assets. Smaller firms are theorized to oppose innovations which reduce net income, even though taxes would be lowered, because of significant implementation costs and possible reductions in incentive compensation. This might explain rejection of revaluation by 88 percent of the French firms, representing only 40 percent of total fixed assets.

Tritschler also studied the adoption of accelerated depreciation and LIFO for tax purposes by U.S. corporations. He found that by 1960, 30 percent of the firms had adopted accelerated depreciation, representing 53 percent of the eligible assets. For the adoption of LIFO, by 1964 only 1.1 percent of manufacturing firms (26 percent of total manufacturing inventory valuation) and 0.43 percent of wholesale and retail firms (5 percent of total merchandising inventory valuation) had made the change. As for the revaluation of assets, it appears that management of the larger companies adopted innovations which enhanced cash flows through tax benefits.

As a result of his findings, Tritschler concluded that the adoption of an innovation is not solely based on a rational analysis of its economic benefits. Behavioral variables involving the compatibility, complexity, trialability, and observability of the change appear to be operant. Asset revaluation, accelerated depreciation, and LIFO may have presented significant implementation problems to smaller potential adopters, and may have been incompatible with their existing systems and norms. The possible tax benefits thus did not outweigh the perceived operational difficulties.

The adoption of LIFO

Ronald Copeland and John Shank (1971) also studied the decision of U.S. firms to use LIFO for tax purposes. They focused on the four change-specific characteristics of relative advantage, compatibility, complexity, and observability, and they hypothesized that each characteristic was weighted equally in the corporation's decision regarding LIFO. Using a survey research approach, questionnaires were completed by the chief financial executives of eighty-six LIFO and ninety-nine nonLIFO corporations concerning the influence of different variables on their LIFO decision. The hypothesis of equal weight was rejected for the LIFO, nonLIFO, and combined samples.

The main finding as identified by Copeland and Shank was that the three behavioral factors emerged as insignificant in comparison to the relative advantage of adopting LIFO. Since, in their opinion, profit maximization could not explain the decision to reject LIFO, Copeland and Shank concluded that behavioral factors were also unable to account for the decision. They accordingly rejected economic and socioeconomic models for describing innovation decisions.

Several criticisms can be lodged against the approach of this study. The hypothesis of equal weights for the relevant variables is arbitrary. More realistic is the expectation that the role of the variables will differ among innovations. Additionally, some bias in the results may have occurred because more of the questions in the research instrument concerned relative advantage than the other characteristics. Even more critical, the questionnaire may have deleted items which would have evoked responses revealing that the behavioral factors were important.

A major defect was Copeland and Shank's failure to consider social structure, cultural values, communication channels, and the many other sociological factors which shape the change environment and influence management's adoption decision (Nash 1971). Also, the positive theory of relative advantage would posit rejection of LIFO by small firms which view the tax benefits as insufficient to counteract the implementation problems and the detrimental effects from reporting lower earnings. Contrary to Copeland and Shank's conclusion, the management of such firms may have been motivated by economic rationality.

Purchase versus pooling of interest

Under profit maximization, or the traditional hypothesis, J. M. Gagnon (1971) suggested management would prefer using pooling of interest accounting for mergers when the price of the acquired company exceeded its book value. Alternatively, the income smoothing hypothesis assumes that managers seek to minimize the discrepancy between normal and current earnings, and use the purchase method for this purpose. Gagnon examined these hypotheses by looking at the number of mergers accounted for as a pooling. For the traditional hypothesis to be supported, the proportion of poolings would increase as pressure is exerted on the accounting profession to relax its restrictions against pooling. However, in periods of rising earnings for firms as a whole (as was the case for the period under study), the income smoothing hypothesis would indicate proportionately more purchases.

Support was found for the traditional hypothesis by looking at the accounting treatment vis-à-vis the price and book value of the acquired company. This led Gagnon to conclude that management will support accounting changes which enhance net income, with detrimental effects (e.g., erosion in guidelines) to pronouncements issued by the accounting profession which tend to depress earnings. (Note that Gagnon's analysis was not concerned with the accounting method used for tax purposes, and his findings are thus difficult to interpret pursuant to the positive theory of relative advantage. Also, the data as reported by Gagnon was insufficient to examine the impact of firm size.)

Installment reporting for tax purposes

In an investigation focused on the adoption of innovations over time, E. E. Comiskey and R. E. Groves (1972) studied the relative importance of the characteristics of installment reporting to those firms which elected to adopt the method for tax purposes. The management of thirty-six large publicly owned department stores were asked to rank thirteen factors by their importance in the adoption decision. A statistically significant consistency in the rankings was found, and seven characteristics emerged as most crucial. Six of the factors related to the relative advantage or economic benefits of using installment reporting for tax purposes, while the remaining characteristic concerned the operational or complexity aspects of the method.

These findings should be analyzed in light of the usual caveats offered regarding survey research, especially the danger of excluding the most important factors from the questionnaire. Additionally, generalizations to all accounting innovations should be made with care, since the characteristics of new practices and procedures differ so widely. But the evidence regarding the importance of relative advantage to the adoption of this particular change is consistent with the findings of previous research.

Accounting for inflation

Mohamed E. A. Hussein (1977) attempted to build and test a theory encompassing the socio-political factors involved in the process of promulgating generally accepted accounting standards. His model contained two elements: (1) the diffusion-of-innovation theory to depict the formulation of accounting standards as a collective innovation adoption decision-making process, and (2) the bargaining interaction model and the mixed power system to describe the resolution of accounting issues as a bargaining exchange for reaching a compromise.

An empirical analysis was performed to study the process of adopting an accounting practice as a generally accepted accounting standard. The following eight characteristics of accounting for inflation were examined to discern their effect on the acceptability of the innovation by all parties involved: relative advantage, relevance, reliability, compatibility, significance, communicability, sufficiency, and practicability. A questionnaire was sent to subjects representing academicians, CPAs, financial analysts, accounting policy makers, and corporate management. A total of fifty-nine responses were used and analyzed.

Evidence was found by Hussein supporting the contention that acceptance of accounting standards is a diffusion-of-innovation process. A "performance gap" was identified wherein the adoption of an innovation is related either to a change in the environment rendering present practices deficient, or to the prospect of a new method being imposed through an accounting policy. New ideas appear to be need stimulated, rather than adopted solely because they are perceived to be superior practices.

In analyzing the importance of the eight characteristics to the adoption of inflation accounting, no statistically significant differences were found between the five subject groups. All parties except financial analysts ranked relevance as the most important factor. The latter group felt reliability was primary. Six additional characteristics were analyzed to determine their correlation with the perceived cost/benefit of accounting for inflation. Generalizations were based on the combined sample and it was found that relevance, radicalness, compatibility, and complexity significantly influenced the expectation of benefits. Verifiability and freedom from bias were important only when absent from the innovation.

It is difficult to derive implications from Hussein's research on the role of characteristics in the acceptability of accounting innovations because of the relatively small sample size and combined analysis of the data. However, this study does support the depiction of accounting policy formulation as a change process.

Replacement-cost disclosures

Corporate management's attitudes toward the provision of replacement costs following the first year of compliance with ASR No. 190 were studied by Lauren Kelly-Newton (1979) to determine management's reaction to the coerced change, and the characteristics of the innovation which influenced that stance. A content analysis was conducted on the general comments section of the replacement cost footnotes in the 1976 10-K annual reports of fifty-three corporations. Sixteen themes were used to categorize the sentences contained within the general comments section, and the frequency of occurrence of the themes was factor analyzed to identify the major concepts within the disclosures.

Seven concepts were identified as representing management's concerns regarding the replacement cost disclosures: (1) accuracy, or imprecision of the data; (2) completeness, or omissions from the information; (3) usefulness, or cautions to users of the disclosures; (4) time, or hypothetical assumptions regarding the future; (5) value, or implications to the book value of the firm; (6) motivation, or management's impetus for disclosing replacement costs; and (7) subjectiveness, or judgments necessary for preparing the data. These concepts largely concern the reliability and relevance of the disclosures, and the negative overtone of the major constructs indicated low attitudinal acceptance of the coerced change.

The concepts can be viewed as manifestations of management's attitudes, and they reveal which characteristics of replacement costs as an innovation were operant in the reactions to ASR No. 190. Both the perception and observability of relative advantages from reporting replacement costs were minimal, as seen in management's concern with the lack of usefulness of the disclosures to financial statement readers and the potential for misuse of the data by such parties. Management's anxiety regarding the reliability of the disclosures was evidenced by the accuracy, completeness, time, and subjectiveness concepts, thus indicating a high perception of complexity in understanding and implementing ASR No. 190. Low compatibility with previous disclosure experiences and financial reporting norms is seen in management's concern with the lack of objectivity in the data. While divisibility was present in the SEC's directive, management's concerns regarding the incompleteness of the data indicate that this was a negative aspect of the innovation.

ALTERNATIVE THEORIES OF MANAGEMENT'S ACCOUNTING POLICY DECISION

Other behavioral explanations have been offered in an attempt to understand the business community's stance toward a change in reporting practices. Four theories have dominated these alternative explanations: income smoothing, functional fixation, learning set, and corporate personality. Examples are given of research relevant to these theories.

Income smoothing

Management's use of alternative accounting methods to smooth net income was first suggested by S. R. Hepworth (1953). (For a comprehensive review of this literature, see Ronen, Sadan, and Snow (1977).) This theory posits management's choice of accounting procedures and their application as attempts to mitigate fluctuations about a normal level of earnings. Smooth income numbers are held implicitly as enhancing the external user's perception of the firm and the assessment of its risks and returns.

Several choices are available to management for achieving a steady income stream. First, the object of smoothing, or the variable to be smoothed, must be chosen; for example, ordinary income or earnings per share. A second factor is the dimension of smoothing: (1) intertemporal as through events occurrence, events recognition, or allocation over time, or (2) classificatory. Third is the smoothing variable, or the instrument to be used to smooth the object variable; for example, depreciation methods and asset lives, pension costs, reporting income from subsidiaries, etc.

Empirical tests of income smoothing activity have relied on examination of financial statements to infer ex post whether management behaved as if it smoothed income. Many studies have sought to identify the presence of smoothing by focusing on various objects, instruments, and norms. Results from this research have only partially supported the hypothesis that management engages in income smoothing behavior.

Functional fixation

The concept of functional fixation was first related to management's reaction to alternative accounting methods by Yuji Ijiri, Robert Jaedicke, and Kenneth Knight (1966). Functional fixation is the phenomenon of ascribing a specific meaning to a title or object and failing to see alternative meanings or uses. It was suggested that functional fixation upon accounting concepts and measurements may explain situations where changes in accounting procedures do not result in adjustments in decision-making processes.

Fixation upon net income on the part of financial statement users would indicate disregard for the accounting methods used in determining the profit figure. Net income as computed with alternative accounting techniques affects only the amount and not the meaning of the concept. If management ascribes to the function-fixation theory, which is akin to assuming financial statement users are naive, opposition will arise to any accounting method which lowers net income, irrespective of a positive impact on the firm's cash flows.

Learning set

A defect of the functional-fixation theory noted by John Livingstone (1967) was its inability to define the factors determining when the presence of alternative accounting methods would impact decisions.

In an extension of function fixation, Livingstone suggested that the existence of a learning set might determine the effect of accounting alternatives. Learning-set theory as applied to accounting suggests that financial statement users will more readily adjust for the effect of new accounting methods if they have prior experience in adapting to accounting alternatives. This indicates the formation of a learning set, where encounters with different problems having similar solutions facilitate recognition of analogous problems and methods of solution.

As a test of this theory, Livingstone studied the impact of alternative tax-allocation methods on rate-of-return decisions made by regulatory agencies for electric utility companies. Livingstone found that regulatory agencies accustomed to dealing with rate bases valued at original cost failed to allow for the effect of alternative tax-allocation methods in determining the common target rate of return. On the other hand, regulatory agencies familiar with reproduction-cost and fair-value rate bases appeared to adjust for the effects of alternative tax allocation methods.

This finding is explained by the failure of original-cost regulatory agencies to formulate a learning set, since they need make no adjustments to the utilities' accounting data in deciding rate cases. Fair-value regulatory agencies frequently make adjustments to the financial information in valuing the rate base. They thus establish a learning set which can be used to make adjustments for different methods of tax allocation.

While this application of the learning set concept focuses on the use of accounting information, it does have implications to the establishment of disclosure policy by corporate management. If financial statement users do formulate learning sets, expanding corporate disclosure such that users could adjust to alternative accounting methods might facilitate learning and lessen functional fixation.

Corporate personality

George Sorter, Selwyn Becker, T. R. Archibald, and William Beaver (1964) observed that a firm's choice of accounting methods could not be explained solely by economic factors. They suggested that corporate personality might influence management's accounting policy decisions. Corporate personality is interpreted as an intolerance for ambiguity, or the need to avoid vague and undefined stimuli. In accounting, this aversion to uncertainty may lead to the computation of a single measure for a particular transaction, regardless of the use of that accounting measurement. Firms with a high intolerance for ambiguity are hypothesized as conservative and averse to risk.

Corporate personality theory was used in an attempt to explain the depreciation methods used by firms for financial reports and income tax purposes. Minimization of tax payment would justify accelerated depreciation for taxable income, while maximization of reported income would call for straight line depreciation for financial reporting. Failure to use two different depreciation methods might be attributed to anxiety over maintaining two sets of accounting records, or an intolerance of ambiguity. As a result, one accounting measure is used for the two separate purposes.

Sorter et al. hypothesized that firms using accelerated depreciation for both income purposes have less conservative corporate personalities than those using straight line depreciation for both purposes, since the former group merely reports lower financial income while the latter group incurs the real cost of higher taxes. Firms using accelerated depreciation for taxable income but straight line depreciation for accounting income should, of course, have even higher tolerance for ambiguity. To test these relationships, the debt/asset ratios, liquid asset positions, attitudes toward controversial accounting issues, and psychological attitudes were studied for a sample of firms from all three groups. Evidence from this investigation supported the contention that the three groups of firms differed in more respects than just depreciation policy, implying the existence of a corporate personality with ramifications to the choice of accounting methods by management.

Corporate personality theory was also used by John Shank and Ronald Copeland (1973) in a study of firms which had made several changes in accounting methods. A comparison of the number of changes during the period from 1966 to 1969 made by this group with those made by a random sample of firms revealed that the first sample made significantly more changes. This provided evidence to Shank and Copeland that a corporate personality exists. Focusing on a specific accounting change, the publication of funds flow statements, they discovered that such "change receptive" companies disclosed these statements earlier than a random sample of firms, further supporting the existence of a behavioral set to the acceptance of change.

The orientation of corporate personality theory differs from that of the concepts previously discussed. In assessing reactions to accounting standards, corporate personality theory stresses the importance of management's motivations and experiences and their influence on tolerance for ambiguity. To enhance the innovation process, corporate personality theory would suggest inculcating a positive attitude to change in management by increasing its experiences with successful changes. Innovation theory, however, focuses on characteristics of the change itself, implying the favorable aspects of the innovation should be magnified to encourage its adoption. Income smoothing, function fixation, and learning-set theory are specifically concerned with management's perception of the relative advantages of a proposed change which accrue from the use of the information. Innovation and corporate personality theories should not be viewed as incompatible and alternative explanations for innovation adoption decisions. Support for a corporate personality does not refute innovation theory, since firms may appear to be "change receptive" when in fact it is the characteristics of the innovation which determine adoption.

Returning to the positive theory of relative advantage, a corporate personality would imply classifying large firms as "change receptive" and small firms as conservative, since the former group supports changes that lower reported earnings while the latter group opposes such innovations. This demonstrates that the characteristics of the innovation as perceived by the individual change target are critical in innovation decisions. If a corporate personality exists, uniform rejection of changes such as revaluation, accelerated depreciation, and LIFO would be unlikely unless firms of similar sizes had similar corporate personalities. To more fully support corporate personality as the major explanatory variable in innovation adoption decisions, individual firms would have to be shown to accept changes possessing dissimilar characteristics.

Chapter Seven

COMPLIANCE WITH ACCOUNTING POLICY

Management's position regarding an accounting policy can take one of two forms: (1) a decision to accept or reject a standard issued by the FASB, or (2) a reaction of support or opposition to an SEC directive. This chapter depicts both these situations as innovation decisions and discusses the nature of those decisions, types of conformity, expression of opposition, and impact of time as influencing factors.

ACCOUNTING INNOVATION DECISIONS

A reaction of support or opposition to an accounting change can be represented by three types of adoption decisions: optional, collective, or authority. Irrespective of the nature of the adoption decision, the same general process is followed in formulating a stance toward the change.

The innovation decision process

An innovation decision is the means by which the change target first learns of a new idea, reaches an accept or reject decision, and conforms overt behavior and/or covert attitudes to that decision. The rate of adoption of an innovation is the length of time over which this decision process occurs.

In reaching an innovation decision or formulating a reaction to a coerced change, different characteristics of the innovation dominate at various stages (Rogers and Shoemaker 1971, p. 160). As management becomes aware of a new accounting practice, the compatibility and complexity of the proposed change are most important. Prior to promulgation of a directive, discussions of the innovation in the academic and professional literature influence the perceptions of these characteristics and help management formulate predispositions. In the early stages of establishing a policy, dissemination of literature to the affected parties by the standard setter fosters understanding of the meaning and use of the proposed change, and enhances the consistency of the innovation with accepted conventions and norms. This stage may involve using persuasion and education strategies.

In the persuasion stage, when the change target is establishing an opinion, relative advantage and observability predominate. Mass media and interpersonal contacts can be used by the policy setter to emphasize the net benefits of the change. Visibility of advantages can be demonstrated by using results from experimental implementation of the innovation. For example, publication of the positive aspects of the AICPA's experimental program for inflation accounting might enhance adoption of that innovation.

Finally, trialability becomes crucial in the decision stage. If management can operationalize the change on a partial basis, it is less apt to feel threatened by an acceptance decision. Suggestions for an incremental approach to policy making and implementation of innovations on an experimental and voluntary basis incorporate this factor, and thus enhance the probability that accounting innovations will be adopted.

Types of adoption decisions

Three types of innovation adoption decisions are possible in establishing a stance to an accounting policy. First is an optional innovation decision, whereby acceptance or rejection of a change is left entirely up to the individual. Individual adoption decisions by the management of a corporation occur when it (1) makes discretionary accounting changes (e.g., switches depreciation methods), or (2) responds to nondiscretionary changes by compliance with or deviation from generally accepted accounting principles as promulgated by the FASB (e.g., capitalization of a lease as required under FAS No. 13) or SEC directives (e.g., nondisclosure of illegal payments). Failure to comply with FASB nondiscretionary changes has implications for the corporation's audit opinion, while deviation from SEC rules may impede the firm's equity market.

Second is a collective innovation decision which involves consensus by all individual members of the social unit. Acceptance by the accounting profession of the FASB as a policy maker is a collective decision, and CPAs have formalized this sanction in their Code of Professional Ethics. Promulgations of new accounting methods by the FASB are accordingly accepted in the accounting profession by the consensus of its members. Positions on proposed changes, such as responses to the FASB's discussion memoranda, are often collective decisions wherein the social unit is an interested party such as a Big Eight accounting firm or an industry group. For example, opposition by small oil and gas producers to FAS No. 19 represented a collective rejection decision.

Finally, an authority innovation decision occurs when someone in a superior power position forces a decision on a second party. Separate groups are responsible for the innovation decision and its adoption; that is, the individual making the decision to change is different from the person who must undergo the change. The decision unit encompasses policy makers with the power to decide whether or not a change should be made, while the adoption unit includes the business sector being forced to implement the innovation. In an individual or collective innovation decision, the policy board attempts to influence management's adoption decision. However, in a coercive situation the standard setter may actually be making the innovation decision. There may be a further distinction between the change agent and the decision unit in a coercive innovation if an external party seeks to influence a power group to mandate a change to a target. This is exemplified by situations wherein the academic community influences the policy directions of the SEC. These situations result in nonmutual goal setting, and although management may not be free to reject the innovation, strong forces of resistance may arise. While authority decisions may enhance the adoption process, the innovation is more apt to be thwarted and subject to discontinuation unless constant surveillance is maintained.

The mandate of an accounting innovation by the SEC exemplifies an authority decision wherein the SEC is accepting or rejecting the idea and the business community is forced to comply. In this case, the SEC must go through an innovation decision process and the affected parties must choose an appropriate response mode. For example, in mandating the disclosure of replacement costs, nonmutual goal setting arose. The SEC's stated objective of communicating information regarding the effect of inflation on the financial condition of corporations to investors was not internalized by the business community.

A critical relationship exists between the type of innovation decision and the change agent's power base. Since the main characteristic of an authority innovation decision is the lack of individual freedom to accept or reject a change, the authority structure of the social system becomes a critical sociological variable. Possessing legitimate power with limited coercion, the FASB lacks the resources to make authority decisions. Thus accounting changes through the private sector rely on individual and collective decisions by management for adoption of proposed innovations. The SEC operates largely from a coercive power base, and it is quite able to make authority decisions. Corporate management will support or oppose those decisions, perhaps in the context of an optional or consensus decision. But inculcation of the change is quite likely due to the authority of the policy maker. On the other hand, when the SEC suggests that corporations adopt a new practice, as in the voluntary disclosure of forecasts, authority decisions are not involved and management is free to make individual and collective decisions.

While a segment of the petroleum industry effectively rejected the FASB's mandate for successful-efforts accounting, the SEC's stronger power base ensures oil and gas producers will comply with its reserve recognition accounting requirements. Since the SEC's method is a variant of inflation accounting, the FASB has been working very closely with the SEC and petroleum industry representatives in developing its inflation reporting requirements. This coordination is intended to mitigate conflict with the SEC's requirements and to avoid collective industry action thwarting the FASB's proposal.

The type of innovation decision is also related to the strategy used by policy makers to encourage adoption. Persuasion and education may be employed in connection with optional, collective, and authoritative decisions. In the first two types of decisions these strategies may be used to foster adoption, while in authority decisions they may focus on encouraging support and lessening opposition from the change target. Resort to a coercive strategy, however, reduces the freedom of the individual or the social system to make an innovation decision, and it usually results in an authority decision. An example of the interaction between strategies and the type of innovation decision is the SEC's initial use of education to enhance optional and collective acceptance of segment reporting, and subsequently its use of coercion in an authority decision to mandate line-of-business disclosure requirements.

An authority innovation decision is clearly distinguished from individual or collective decisions by the strong role of the policy maker, and the innovation decision process is affected accordingly. In all three types of adoption decisions, the impetus for a change usually initiates with the policy board which becomes aware of a problem area and/or a desirable accounting innovation. In an authority decision, the standard setter then enters the persuasion stage and evaluates the innovation through an assessment of its ability to solve the problem, expected costs, feasibility of implementation, probable consequences, and business community reaction. In developing the SEC's replacement-cost accounting requirements, this evaluative stage was spearheaded by former Chief Accountant John C. Burton, who conceptually accepted the need for replacement cost disclosures.

The innovation adoption decision may be totally authoritative, in which the decision is made unilaterally by the standard setter, or participative, in which corporate management is involved in the final resolution. By allowing for genuine two-way communication, a participative authority innovation decision has a greater chance of being positively received by the business community. Communication of the decision necessitates that the policy setter familiarize corporations with the directive, including the desired meaning to be imparted regarding the innovation. Intermediaries more adept in communicating with management may be employed to encourage acceptance of the innovation, such as CPAs who function as opinion leaders. Management formally enters the innovation process only at the adoption stage in which the change is implemented and behavior is modified. In an authority innovation, compliance is most likely to result. Overt action does not imply, however, that complying firms agree with implementation of the innovation.

The decision to use authority

Coercive innovations typically occur in formal organizations characterized by predetermined goals, prescribed roles, an authority structure, and rules and regulations. The existence of a formal structure does not imply the predominance of authority innovation decisions, since those in a power position might instead attempt to influence individual or collective innovation decisions. For example, the SEC uses coercion to force some accounting changes, but leaves other innovations to optional and collective decisions by delegating its standard setting power to the FASB or issuing voluntary regulations.

Certain aspects of the innovation situation can be seen as encouraging the use of authority (Zaltman and Duncan 1977, pp. 153–160). A power strategy may be appropriate if the objective of the standard setter is to obtain short-term behavioral change without attitudinal acceptance. This might be applicable in a situation where an immediate remedial solution is needed for a pressing condition, as when the amount of time available to effect the change is short. Policy setters must determine the degree of commitment to the innovation by the business community which is desired, as changes which are to be maintained without continual interference or surveillance usually require some amount of persuasion and education.

Since coercive innovations depend on monitoring activities and the granting of rewards and punishments, policy makers must assess the cost and benefits associated with exercising authority. Programs of surveillance and punishment are expensive to enact, while less tangible costs arise if the business community opposes a mandated change. Benefits from authority innovation decisions accrue to society as a whole, since such actions are aimed at eliminating a social problem. Thus the benefits to an accounting policy maker from issuing a directive relate to the fulfillment of its expected role, usually stated as enhancing the public interest. Prior to exercising its authority, the change agent should consider whether the potential benefits from forcing an innovation outweigh the expected costs.

When an authority innovation decision is made, the business community must be able to both accept and sustain the innovation. If resources are not available for enacting the change, and the change agent does not supply them, a coercive innovation will have detrimental effects on the target social system. Continuation of the change also requires adequate resources. Forced compliance may be indicated if the corporate community possesses limited resources and resists using them to adopt the innovation.

Corporate management's felt need to change its financial reporting practices influences the use of coercion. If this need is low and a lack of time precludes the use of persuasion or education, an authority innovation decision may be imperative. Even if management believes a change is justified, however, there may be opposition to the policy setter's suggested solution. If resistance to the innovation is expected, an authority decision may be effective for rapidly enacting the change and minimizing resistance before programs of opposition are organized. If accounting policy setters know corporate management will not voluntarily adopt an innovation, as may be indicated during a program of persuasion or education, coercion may be the only recourse. Where specific groups or industries are seen as opposing a change, a power strategy may be necessary for only that segment of the change target. Given a situation of significant resistance, particularly where the benefits from adopting the change are not highly visible to the business community, the policy board may decide that actual experience with the innovation will sufficiently demonstrate its advantages and favorably influence the corporate community to attitudinally accept the idea. The standard setter would accordingly mandate the change.

The characteristics of the innovation also influence when an authority innovation decision is appropriate. In general, when an innovation is deficient in the qualities that foster voluntary adoption, a power strategy may be necessary. If the change is compatible with management's values, perceived as possessing significant relative advantages, and has benefits that are highly communicable, a persuasive strategy may be quite effective. A very complex change may necessitate the use of education, and insufficient implementation and conceptual guidance with an authority innovation decision may contribute to rejection or significant resistance. If the innovation is divisible, a power strategy may be appropriate for its initial trial. Working in consort, these factors determine the magnitude of the change to the corporate community, and indicate the extent to which power will be needed to obtain compliance.

The SEC's mandate for replacement-cost disclosures can be scrutinized within this framework to ascertain whether an authority innovation decision was needed. It is doubtful that the SEC was merely interested in immediate behavioral changes, concerned only with forced disclosure of replacement costs dependent on surveillance. Instead, the SEC appeared intent on fostering long-run reforms in financial reporting which would be acceptable to both management and financial statement users. This objective coincides with its fundamental goal of ensuring adequate disclosure for investors. The SEC at least implicitly decided that replacement-cost information is important enough to financial statement users to warrant additional administrative expenses and possible costs from corporate resistance.

To maintain the disclosure of replacement costs by corporations without SEC surveillance necessitates attitudinal acceptance by the business community. While the SEC did enact a period of experimentation to increase familiarity with and knowledge of replacement costs, resistance to ASR No. 190 revealed this program was insufficient. This decreases the likelihood that the SEC can achieve anything beyond short-run behavioral compliance for the disclosure of replacement costs. Corporations estimated compliance with ASR No. 190 would be costly. However it was clear that internal staff and outside experts were available to determine the information. Since many of the reporting expenses were first-time costs, the burden from continued compliance was lower. In considering the business community's ability to adopt the innovation, the real issue appeared to be management's opposition to using its limited resource, internal personnel, to estimate replacement costs. This represented a high opportunity cost to most corporations.

The attributes of replacement-cost accounting which contributed to opposition by corporate management reduced the likelihood that individual or collective innovation decisions would favor adoption. A delay in issuing ASR No. 190 might have allowed time for the corporate community to become increasingly opposed and to organize formal plans for resisting the disclosure of replacement costs or for challenging the SEC's power. An authority innovation decision with relatively rapid passage of ASR No. 190 may have been appropriate in this situation for halting more severe opposition.

The divisibility of replacement-cost accounting as an innovation indicates that coerced change may have been suitable for its initial trial. Although many complaints were lodged against ASR No. 190 because of its partial approach to inflation accounting, mandating comprehensive current value disclosures with price-level adjustments for monetary items might have intensified opposition. The SEC may also have determined that experience with disclosing replacement costs would lessen initial opposition to the innovation. Additionally, it was clear that ASR No. 190 would represent a change of significant magnitude to complying firms. Given the nature of the environment, the characteristics of replacement costs as an innovation, the large number of parties to be affected, and the obvious resistance, the use of authority may have been quite appropriate, and even necessary, to procure the disclosure of replacement costs.

CONFORMITY TO ACCOUNTING POLICY

Management's ultimate reaction to an accounting standard can include a behavioral reaction involving changes in reporting practices and/or an attitudinal response involving modifications in predispositions to the idea.

Behavioral compliance

Overt acceptance by corporate management of an accounting change suggested or mandated by a policy setter can be observed through scrutiny of the firm's financial disclosures. This level of conformity involves modification of behavior. In addition to the characteristics of an innovation, two aspects of the policy maker's power base influence the likelihood of overt compliance: the strength and range of power.

First, the strength of the change agent's power suggests that possession of coercive power, such that authority decisions can be made, almost ensures behavioral compliance. A coercive strategy will be unsuccessful and the innovation will not be adopted if insufficient power is wielded over the business community in the area to be affected. The strength of the policy setter's power is a function of management's dependency on that group for achievement of its objectives, which in turn depends on the goals controlled, their importance to management, other means for satisfaction of the goals, and the cost of using alternatives.

The FASB's authority is limited by a theoretical power imbalance between the business community and the accounting profession (Goldman and Barlev 1974). A firm is free to select its auditor from among a large body of CPAs and to disengage any particular accountant when desired. Veiled or open threats regarding the employment of the accountant provide the corporation with significant influence over the auditor's activities. While the business community is dependent on the CPA profession for the performance of the audit function, the routine nature of the activity means the power of any one specific CPA firm does not emanate from auditing services. Corporations may "shop around" in pursuit of more lenient CPAs who are willing to issue an unqualified report for a particular infraction. Strengthening of the power of CPAs to at least the level of behavioral compliance is attributable to the AICPA's Code of Professional Ethics, audit committees, accounting policy reducing flexibility, and increased legal liability to third parties.

The SEC's power to secure compliance with its directives stems largely from management's desire to have the firm's registration statement accepted and public trading of its securities continue uninterrupted. The SEC has direct control over this goal, since management's only option other than following the SEC's requirements is to seek alternative equity sources such as debt. This may be a costly or infeasible choice. The SEC's requirements that a registrant's audit opinion be unqualified and changes in auditors be disclosed strengthens the power of the accounting profession. Sanction of the private sector's accounting principles enhances behavioral conformity to such standards at least in the firm's filings with the SEC. Compliance with SEC regulations in those reports is, of course, virtually assured.

The strength of coercive power is related to two factors which are critical for obtaining behavioral conformity: the magnitude of the negative effects from punishment and the perceived probability that punishment can be avoided through compliance (French and Raven 1960). While the ultimate outcome of failure to follow SEC reporting requirements is highly undesirable, the SEC's coercive power is reduced if corporations do not feel disciplinary proceedings are likely. Management will form its perception of the chances of negative sanctions by assessing both the SEC's surveillance activities through its review of corporate filings, and the SEC's punishment actions for deficient filings. Looking at the overall change environment, while the source of power and its legitimacy are seen as important, the extent to and conditions under which it is used emerge as the actual determinants of the strength and effectiveness of that power.

The second aspect of the policy maker's power base, the range of power, suggests that regardless of the strength of the policy board's power, it is limited in range to those aspects of behavior which can be controlled. Consideration must also be given to the ability of the change target to completely withdraw from the policy setter's range of power. If such a reaction is feasible, the strength of power is diminished. The range within which the power is effective must be carefully defined, and controls must be adequate to ensure the business community cannot easily escape this range.

Having received sanction by the SEC through ASR No. 150 to establish accounting standards for reporting to the SEC, the FASB's range of power was significantly extended beyond corporate annual reporting. The SEC's directives, however, generally apply only to reporting under the 1933 and 1934 Acts, and management often deletes some of the detailed disclosures from its annual stockholder reports. For example, while the SEC required corporations to mention in their reports to stockholders that replacement costs were disclosed in their 10-K annual reports, very few corporations voluntarily provided the actual amounts in the stockholder annual reports since the inclusion of the data was not required.

Attitudinal acceptance

Effectiveness of a policy board should not be judged solely by whether the business community modified its reporting practices. A common misconception is that once behavioral conformity has been obtained, the standard setter has been successful in gaining acceptance of the innovation (Chin and Benne 1972). This viewpoint ignores the importance of the covert state and its relationship to overt actions. While corporations complied with requirements of FAS No. 8 to recognize realized and unrealized foreign exchange gains and losses in current net income, severe opposition demonstrated the lack of covert acceptance of the standard. The FASB's actions to amend FAS No. 8 represent admission of the failure of the directive, even though overt compliance was obtained.

In an optional or collective innovation decision, attitudinal acceptance by the change target is frequently a part of the decision process and a precondition to adoption. In an authority decision, covert acceptance lessens resistance to coerced changes. In all cases, genuine acceptance of an innovation by management involves educational programs regarding the nature of the change and its implementation, as well as a refocus of attitudes and values and possibly a modification in social system relationships. Attitudinal conformity with internalization of norms should be sought to enhance compatibility between management's values and overt actions, regardless of the extent of coercion involved. Additionally, covert acceptance should not be sought without consideration of the characteristics of an innovation which influence its adoption.

An authority innovation decision which invokes initial resistance may actually lead to subsequent acceptance as a consequence of that opposition (Walton 1965). This may result from innovation dissonance, or a discrepancy between management's attitude toward an innovation and the forced adoption or rejection of that change. Figure 7-1 shows four possible dissonant-consonant types. The arrows indicate the pressures toward consonance. Management will attempt to establish a position of equilibrium, or consonance, such that attitudes are consistent with behavior (Types I and IV). Balance theory of tension reduction implies that dissonance cannot be maintained over the long run. Once in a dissonant situation (Types II and III), management will attempt to move toward consonance by either (1) changing its attitudes such that they conform with the forced behavior, or (2) changing its overt behavior through discontinuation, misuse, or circumvention of the innovation.

The SEC's 1976 proposal to require the filing of forecasts if projections are made to outsiders created a situation of dissonant adoption. Financial executives' decision to cease all forecasting activity revealed that equilibrium would be established through consonant re-

Figure 7-1
Dissonant-consonant types based on attitudinal and behavior compliance

Change Target Attitude Toward the Innovation	Overt Behavior Forced By the Change Agent	
	Rejection	Adoption
Unfavorable	I Consonant Rejector ←	II Dissonant Adopter
	↑	↑
Favorable	III Dissonant Rejector →	IV Consonant Adopter

Reprinted with permission of Macmillan Publishing Co., Inc., from *Communication of Innovations* by Everett M. Rogers and F. Floyd Shoemaker. Copyright © 1971 by The Free Press, a Division of Macmillan Publishing Co., Inc.

jection; that is, management would avoid being subject to the requirements (Foster 1978, pp. 538-539). Replacement-cost accounting as mandated under ASR No. 190 established a strong condition of dissonant adoption on the part of corporations. While some indication can be found of a lessening in this initial resistance and movement toward consonant adoption (McLagan and Ross 1977), evidence also exists of attempts to undermine the effectiveness of the innovation. (See the subsequent section, Opposition to Accounting Standards.)

Rather than placing management in a dissonant condition, policy setting through coercion should begin with attempts to modify attitudes and values such that when introduced, the change is compatible with the business community's norms. A priori consideration should be given to whether dissonance will be created, and if so, whether management will attempt to establish equilibrium through a modification of attitudes or circumvention of the innovation. Dissonance theory influences the consequence analysis conducted prior to the formulation of an authority innovation decision. The SEC presumably considered such factors when it realized that coerced forecasting would result in circumvention of the rule, and it accordingly rescinded the proposal.

Additionally, once a coercive innovation is enacted, management's attitudes toward the change should be monitored over time to determine how balance will be established. If the policy setter finds attitudinal acceptance is not forthcoming, revocation of the forced change should be seriously considered, since management will engage in attempts to thwart its effectiveness. Because overt behavior is manipulated by the policy maker in a coercive power strategy, the business community's attitude toward the innovation is an important determinant of the long-run success of the innovation. This fact was recognized by the SEC Advisory Committee on Corporate Disclosure (1977, pp. 336-338) when it urged the SEC to establish formalized procedures for studying the consequences which result from its directives.

While dissonance theory primarily relates to the formulation of policy through coercion, the principles are applicable to standard setters possessing legitimate power coupled with a high degree of authority. For example, many of the FASB's policies create initial conditions of dissonant adoption (e.g., interim recognition of foreign currency translation gains and losses pursuant to FAS No. 8), and dissonant rejection (e.g., prohibitions against the use of pooling of interest as contained in APB Opinion No. 16). Management's attempts to establish consonance often involve circumvention of the rules by finding loopholes in the standards or employing CPAs who do not insist upon compliance.

The alternatives available to management in a dissonant situation can be analyzed within the context of information inductance, whereby information dissemination requirements affect the behavior of the information sender (Prakash and Rappaport 1977). Three types of effects are indicated: (1) modification in the description of performance, by either choosing from alternative accounting methods or altering the information in an unacceptable manner such that commissions or omissions result; (2) modifying de facto behavior as by conforming behavior to expectations; and (3) modifying objectives. Given an initial position of dissonant adoption, the first effect represents circumvention or consonant rejection, while the latter two effects involve consonant adoption.

OPPOSITION TO ACCOUNTING STANDARDS

In the course of reaching an innovation decision, or as a consequence of a coercive innovation, the business community may express dissatisfaction with the change. Resistance is heightened when the innovation is seen as possessing low relative advantages, presenting significant implementation problems, contradicting existing value schemes, or lying outside the policy maker's range of power. Greater perceptions of negative characteristics and more entrenched norms result in stronger opposition. Expressions of hostility usually take one of two general forms: (1) attacks on the innovation through public statements regarding the importance of the issue, campaigns to demonstrate opposition to the coerced change, and attempts to thwart the objective to be accomplished by the innovation, or (2) attacks on the change agent through attempts to build political and economic power against the policy maker and challenges to the legitimacy, authority, and coercive power of the standard setter.

Criticism of the innovation

The first form of opposition focuses on attempts to undermine the proposed change and the policy board's objectives, and may involve circumventing the requirements of the directive. An example is the previously cited reaction by the business community to the SEC's 1976 proposal to mandate disclosure of forecasts if such projections were made informally to outsiders. Management stated it would cease forecasting activity rather than be subject to the SEC's requirements. This reaction is also found where accounting standards are highly complex, allowing management to find loopholes in the requirements. The highly technical nature of lease accounting pursuant to FAS No. 13 encourages lessees to structure the conditions of a lease agreement such that it does not meet the criteria of a capital lease.

The business community may also embark on campaigns to publicize the defects and disadvantages of a policy in the financial press. Strong resentment by management to replacement cost disclosure requirements was voiced prior to actual experience in complying with ASR No. 190. (See, for example, "Corporations Doubt Usefulness of Replacement Cost Data, Survey Shows" (1976); Carlson (1977); and DeWelt (1977).) Many of the objections revolved around the questionable use of the data. Other critics bemoaned the difficulties of complying with the requirements, calling the mandate a nightmare to accountants and faulting it for requiring open experimentation.

Direct attacks on the utility of the data were contained within the replacement-cost footnote itself in general statements by management concerning the adequacy of the information (Kelly-Newton 1979; see also Arthur Young & Co. (1977)). Scrutiny of these disclosures revealed that seven general concepts were stressed: the data were inaccurate, incomplete, subjective, not useful, not representative of future expectations, not reflective of value to stockholders, and provided solely to comply with SEC requirements. The expression of these concerns was also found in firms' annual reports to stockholders where firms stated that replacement costs were disclosed in their 10-K annual reports. (See Bastable (1977).) Attempts to undermine the SEC's goal of providing useful information to investors were thus made by management through derogatory statements in the actual replacement-cost footnotes. Stressing the deficiencies of the disclosures, the business community campaigned against the use of the data, and may have hoped investors would join in opposition to ASR No. 190. Management believed it had accomplished its goal of detracting from the utility of replacement cost disclosures as revealed by the following survey finding: "Other respondents felt that the disclaimers and qualifications issued by most firms in conjunction with their reporting of replacement costs made the data virtually useless to readers" (Garsombke 1978, p. 26).

Discrediting the value of new information within the disclosure itself was also contemplated by corporations as a possible response to the SEC's 1973 proposal for reporting forecasts (Carpenter and Daily 1974, p. 74). Management indicated that forecasts disclosed in annual reports would be more conservative than those used internally by the firm, and that the reported forecasts might be so hedged that their utility to financial statement users would be destroyed.

Challenges to the policy maker

The second form of opposition involves sanctions against the policy board in its role as a change agent. Aversion to an innovation, especially when the change is coerced through an authority innovation decision, often results in decreased respect for the policy maker by the business community. Such negative feelings can easily spread to the range over which the standard setter exercises power and to the policy board itself. Any referent power that the policy maker as a change agent might possess, resulting in business community identification with the policy setter, is accordingly diminished.

Erosion of the APB's credibility has been attributed to management's vent of dissatisfaction through attacks on the APB's authority:

> [the business community] issued press releases denouncing the APB, published briefs, circulated white papers, threatened to sue the APB, petitioned the SEC, asked the FPC for a ruling, sought Treasury Department intervention, asked Congress to put financial reporting flexibility into law (Moonitz 1974, p. 85).

Challenges to the SEC's authority were made in response to ASR No. 190. The replacement cost disclosure requirement was cited as an extension of the SEC's traditional "watchdog" role and the SEC was accused of using a "steamroller" approach and being guilty of "activism at its worst" (Carlson 1977; Bastable 1977, p. 75).

The interacting forces can be studied within a decentralized structure for policy making whereby Congress delegates authority for establishing accounting standards to the SEC, which in turn delegates this responsibility to the FASB (Horngren 1972). The customers of the system are defined as those parties affected by the standards including management, accountants, and financial statements users. Opposition to directives will be directed to the agency responsible for delegating its authority: Congress for complaints regarding the SEC, and the SEC for dissatisfaction with the FASB. If the higher authority decides the standards are adequate, corporate management will be thwarted in its opposition, and the policy maker's (delegated) authority will remain intact. Strong incentives exist, however, for Congress in particular to pay close attention to complaints from affected parties, since in the final analysis these groups can replace Congress itself through the voting mechanism. Although largely politically motivated rather than based on complaints from third parties, Congressional responsibility for the public interest may at least partially explain recent investigations into the accounting profession and the activities of the SEC and FASB, resulting in identification of deficiencies by the late Senator Lee Metcalf relating to the SEC's delegation of its responsibility for establishing accounting standards to the private sector.

Consistent with this paradigm, the most severe mechanism for expressing dissatisfaction are challenges to the policy board's authority. When the business community objects to a proposed change, it must decide whether or not to stay within the system. One of the first examples of this type of challenge occurred in 1959, when three corporations sought an injunction against a letter of clarification of ARB No. 44 (Revised) issued by the CAP (Zeff 1972, pp. 166–167; 1978, p. 58; Savoie 1974, pp. 325–326). While the companies were ruled against in two courts, a precedent was established for the use of an appeal mechanism by dissatisfied parties. Other challenges to the APB's authority followed: complaints to Congress regarding indications that pooling-of-interest accounting for business combinations might be eliminated, petitions for Congressional intervention to forestall the disallowance of the flow-through method of accounting for the investment tax credit, insurance industry appeals to the SEC in opposition to the market value approach to accounting for marketable securities, petitions to Congress and the SEC by oil and gas producers opposing successful-efforts accounting, and lobbying in Congress by leasing companies to forestall mandatory capitalization of leases.

The critical role of vested interests and the possible detrimental effects on policy makers is seen in the following observation of the investment tax credit episode:

Attitudes displayed here plainly indicate that some businessmen and professional accountants wanted to destroy the APB if that was necessary to have their own way on the investment credit. If the same people were removed from the emotional issue of the investment credit, most of them would probably be strong supporters of standard-setting in the private sector (Savoie 1974, p. 326).

Nor has the FASB been immune from such attacks, having learned first hand that challenges to its authority through government and SEC involvement arise from business community opposition. The mandate of successful-efforts accounting for oil and gas producing companies initiated lobbying activities in Congress to allow the continued use of alternative accounting methods, an aborted legislative attempt to enact such flexibility into law, a series of public hearings by the SEC and Department of Energy, and ultimate rejection of the FASB's policy by the SEC. While this action by the SEC severely injured the FASB's credibility, the FASB itself recognized that the activities that preceded the overrule of FAS No. 19 had serious implications for the FASB's authority position: "But repeated demands on Congress and the various federal departments and agencies to negate self-regulatory decisions fairly and properly arrived at within the private sector may tend to erode the private sector's capability to regulate itself" (FAF, FASB 1978, p. 12).

Serious challenges have also been made to the SEC's authority ("Arthur Andersen Sues SEC" 1976). In 1976, the Big Eight accounting firm of Arthur Andersen & Company filed a petition with the SEC asking that ASR Nos. 150 and 177 be revoked. Rejection of this petition by the SEC led Arthur Andersen & Company to seek a court injunction prohibiting the SEC from enforcing these rules. Arthur Andersen & Company contended that delegation of authority for standard setting pursuant to ASR No. 150 was illegal, and requirements that CPAs state whether accounting changes are to "preferable" methods as contained in ASR No. 177 are discriminatory and beyond the SEC's authority. Arthur Andersen & Company was unsuccessful in its attempts to forestall the SEC's requirements, but its attack hurt the credibility of the SEC during Congressional investigations.

While the Arthur Andersen & Company challenge was made by an accounting firm and not the business community, it received at least implicit support by the management of Arthur Andersen & Company's clients. In defiance of ASR No. 177, Arthur Andersen & Company stated that accounting changes by its clients were to "acceptable" rather than "preferable" accounting practices. Presumably these firms concurred with the inclusion of such statements in their filings and were prepared to suffer the consequences. In one instance a company received a deficiency letter for this action, and in a second case the SEC refused to clear a firm's registration statements.

The potency of formal challenges to a policy maker's authority has been recognized in statements opposing the replacement-cost disclosure requirements. In a stinging indictment of the SEC's issuance of ASR No. 190, one critic faults the business community for inertia:

> Given the dissatisfaction of American business with replacement cost disclosure, perhaps the most significant aspect is the absence of any indication that rule 3-17 is to be challenged in the courts. This speaks volumes on the extent to which American business is conditioned to regulation, no matter how costly or bad (Bastable 1977, p. 76).

Whether restricted to grumblings against requirements and attempts to circumvent rules, or extended to challenges against a policy setter's overall authority, the net result of such opposition and hostility is to weaken the chances of successfully implementing a change, including both behavioral and attitudinal conformity. Such failure will occur regardless of the normative "correctness" of an innovation.

ACCOUNTING CHANGES OVER TIME

A final element in management's innovation decision process is the effect of time on gaining acceptance of policies. An individual manager's innovativeness, or the time by which an innovation is adopted relative to the business community, is pertinent in individual and collective decisions and may be used to gauge expected responses to authority decisions. Research has suggested that adoption of an innovation over time follows a normal distribution, with a small group of early adopters and laggards at the beginning and end of the life cycle of the innovation, respectively (Rogers and Shoemaker 1971, pp. 177-179). This pattern may be due to learning effects from experience with the innovation and diffusion, or pressure on individuals as more members of the social system adopt the innovation.

Correspondingly, in a coercive innovation decision, resistance may diminish as experience is gained with the new idea. Modifications in attitudes will be enhanced if net benefits are found to accrue from adoption. Such changes in attitudes result from alterations in the meaning of an innovation and its use as diffusion proceeds. Early adopters may hold different perceptions regarding the attributes of the innovation than late adopters, and management's impression of an accounting innovation may change after adoption. The dynamic nature of these attitudes heightens the importance of ascertaining the perceptions of a new idea at the time of the innovation decision, and monitoring these attitudes over the innovation's life. The diffusion process, whereby the innovation spreads throughout the business community, can then be used to enhance the policy-setting mechanism.

A study of the adoption distribution over time of four accounting innovations implemented by thirty-six large publicly owned department stores revealed a normally-distributed curve described the adoption of two accounting practices—sales on the installment method and revolving credit sales (Comiskey and Groves 1972). The adoption over time of installment reporting for tax purposes and accelerated depreciation for tax purposes was not found to be normally distributed. Conceptually, a normal distribution could be expected, with deviations anticipated as the circumstances surrounding each innovation differ. Accelerated depreciation for tax purposes may be subject to a faster rate of adoption since it is not complex, and has greater relative advantages and highly visible benefits. Because each innovation possesses different characteristics and the perceptions of these attributes vary, adoption over time should be studied on a multi-dimensional scale rather than being solely related to the passage of time.

This alternative explanation overlooks the fact that the attributes of the innovation can influence the dispersion of the curve without necessarily affecting its shape. For example, an innovation with characteristics perceived as favorable and thus fostering adoption could have a very small standard deviation, corresponding to rapid implementation with very few early or late adopters. An innovation with less favorable attributes could have a flatter distribution with the peak of adoption coming much later. Of course, skewed distributions could also be expected, depicting the influence of different attributes and sociological factors.

The influence of time and the hypothesized relationships in the diffusion process are probably most useful for guiding the policy maker's monitoring activities. Knowledge that attitudes change over time may forestall hasty revocation of a standard. For example, resistance to replacement-cost disclosures may lessen as managers become more adept in their computation, find the costs of compliance are not as onerous as feared, do not suffer legal liability for inaccurate projections, and observe their utility for internal and external decision making. A model of adoption over time will also indicate to the policy maker when a change is not being implemented as expected, and encourage reconsideration of directives to which substantial resistance remains.

SUMMARY

Voluntary adoption of an FASB accounting standard by management or formulation of an opinion regarding an SEC directive by the business community were depicted as innovation decisions. The characteristics of a proposed change are influencing factors at various stages of the decision-making process. Of the three types of innovation decisions, individual and collective decisions are made by the accounting profession and business community, while authority decisions are made by the SEC.

Compliance with an accounting standard can take the form of behavioral conformity and/or attitudinal acceptance. Overt behavioral changes depend on the strength and range of the policy setter's power, while covert approval is vital to long-run acceptance of the innovation. Innovation dissonance describes the relationship between attitudes and behavior, particularly in a coercive innovation, and pressures toward establishing consonance determine the ultimate outcome from a directive.

Management's opposition to a proposed or enacted standard can take two general forms: criticism of the innovation itself or attacks on the policy maker. Attempts to discredit the proposed change may involve evasion of the reporting requirements as well as public statements discrediting the change and the utility of the information, possibly resulting in an impairment of the policy board's objectives. Challenges to the standard setter may involve petitions to higher levels of authority to enact sanctions, with a general loss of credibility emerging.

The adoption of innovations over time may be theoretically distributed as a normal curve. The influence of attributes specific to each change and other sociological variables may be responsible for deviations from this pattern.

Chapter Eight

A REEXAMINATION OF ACCOUNTING POLICY MAKING

The formulation of reporting and disclosure standards for external financial accounting has been examined from the context of its broad societal role. The purpose of this chapter is to integrate the many intervening factors into a policy-making process which facilitates the acceptance of change. The implications of the model to the various parties involved with accounting standards are also considered.

THE IMPORTANCE OF A SOCIOLOGICAL PERSPECTIVE

The formulation of accounting standards has been recognized increasingly as a social activity. Directives from policy makers on measurement and disclosure issues for external financial reporting affect the economic welfare of both financial statement users and preparers. Real resource changes result as investors' decisions are influenced by the resulting financial statements, and corporate management's actions are swayed by the effect on the firm's external reports. This larger role of accounting disclosures has led to consideration of the economic consequences of accounting standards, wherein the impact of measurement and disclosure requirements on decision makers who both use and provide accounting information are recognized.

Impact analysis can be narrowed to focus on the importance of accounting standards to corporate management as the supplier of financial information. Management's interest in accounting standards emanates from an agency theory of the corporation, wherein management as an agent acts on behalf of the shareholders or principals of the firm. This relationship establishes the incentives in the market mechanism that motivate management's concern with financial reporting requirements.

Recognition that management can no longer be ignored in the formulation of accounting policy establishes the need for a broader approach to the resolution of controversial issues for enhanced policy making. Identification of the aspects of any given issue that are important to the corporate community fosters an understanding of the political nature of the policy process. The relevant social and political variables can be interrelated within a sociological framework for the establishment of accounting policy. Consideration must be given to such variables, as they establish the appropriate role for management within the framework.

In providing information pursuant to its function as an agent, management's reactions to accounting standards can be assessed in terms of whether a directive has a substantive impact on the firm. Accounting policies with a substantive impact result in real economic changes for the entity, with direct effects on stockholder wealth. These real economic impacts can occur from two types of standards. First, an accounting policy may result in new disclosures which represent additional information to the equity market. Investment decisions may be changed in response to such disclosures, resulting in changes in the firm's stock prices, and an impact on shareholder and management wealth. This effect occurs in the absence of an immediate cash flow impact on the firm. New disclosures that also affect cash flows lead to additional adjustments in equity prices, as the expectation of future cash flows is altered.

Second, an accounting policy may simply change the form of disclosure without providing new information. If, however, there is an immediate impact on the firm's cash flows, changes in expectations will affect current stock prices. Both of the avenues leading to a real economic impact on the firm provide the impetus for management to become actively involved in the policy-making process.

The absence of a direct economic effect does not preclude a reaction by management to an accounting standard. Two situations may arise where accounting policies which have no immediate cash flow impact and do not result in additional disclosures still invoke corporate interest. First, placing high importance on accounting numbers, especially the earnings figure, encourages concern with any standard that changes that measure. This importance may occur in several ways. If management believes investors naively and myopically make decisions based on reported income, it may expect an impact on its equity markets from an accounting standard which affects only the reporting format. Management would also resist attempts to reduce its flexibility for "signalling" financial statement users through accounting disclosures. Basing compensation contracts on accounting numbers fosters high managerial interest in accounting procedures. Additionally, if monitoring arrangements are formulated on financial accounting standards, a change in reporting requirements may affect bonding agreements, causing unwarranted scrutiny of management's activities.

Second, even if an immediate impact on cash flows is lacking, the potential for such an impact may incite reactions to a nonsubstantive issue. This potential effect may derive from expected changes in tax policy, anticipated regulatory actions, future political costs, and additional bookkeeping expenses. Expectations regarding these effects may cause changes in assessments of the firm's future cash flows, thus affecting current stock prices, and shareholder and management wealth.

Whether or not a policy is expected to have a real economic effect on the firm (i.e., result in a substantive or nonsubstantive impact), many factors exist which motivate management to react to a specific directive. These reactions influence the role management should assume in formulating policy, and thus imply viewing that role within the context of planned social change.

A POLICY-MAKING MODEL

Given the need to consider the broader role of accounting policy, a model for the functional resolution of controversial issues can be developed within the framework of planned social change. Figure 1-1 in Chapter 1 depicts the major elements of the model. In formulating this paradigm, it is important that the influences of corporate management and the policy maker be identified and integrated into the framework at their critical points. The policy-making process follows the framework for engineering change through accounting policy as previously developed. Major inputs to this process include the policy setter's power position, aspects of the policy which influence management's reaction, and the nature of business community compliance. The critical output that affects the ultimate standard is the strategy adopted by the policy maker.

The model for effective formulation of accounting policy begins with identification of a financial reporting situation in need of change.

While the desire for a change may emanate from any interested party, a policy board must concur and formulate a suggested solution. Acceptance of the proposed change is enhanced if the need for a modification in corporate disclosures is instilled within the business community.

A second important element is the acceptance of the policy maker as a change agent. The receptiveness of corporate management to the FASB and SEC is influenced by the sensitivity of these policy boards to the social and political aspects of their decisions. The process followed by accounting standard setters in formulating policy indicates their awareness of outside interests and affects corporate approval of their status as change agents. Failure to garner acceptance as a change agent may ultimately result in the demise of the policy board.

An input to establishing the credibility of the standard setter is its position of power within the accounting environment. Coercive power, as possessed by the SEC, can be used to counterbalance corporate opposition to a change agent. With direct authority to mediate punishment for deviant behavior, resistance to directives issued by the coercive policy setter is minimized and the power base is strengthened. Reliance on legitimate power, as by the FASB, is strengthened by the delegation of authority from a more powerful policy board and the support from outside parties. Lacking coercive power, the corporate community must accept the standard setter as holding a sanctioned right to enact change. This weaker power position opens the potential for lower acceptance of the policy maker as a change agent. Since two policy boards exist to formulate accounting standards, their relative power positions are also important to their authority. Disagreement over the resolution of controversial issues or promulgation of conflicting policies lessens the credibility of the policy boards.

Next in the process of issuing a standard is attenuation to outsiders' views, including management's customs and norms in financial reporting. Critical to effectively considering these views are the communication channels established for incorporating corporate input into the policy deliberations. The formulation of a formal rule-making process precludes the use of ad hoc and capricious actions which neglect the views of outside parties. Broad representation of the policy board's constituents by membership on its committees and decision-making groups insures the business community has an opportunity to be heard and impact final decisions. Documents issued at all stages of the process that invite feedback on the proposed change allow for input by all interested parties. Communication is also enhanced through public hearings which permit formal presentation of opinions. Considering research findings on a given topic which result from studies conducted outside the policy board fosters a broader consideration of the issues. While all these techniques allow for considerable input to the policy maker of the reactions of outsiders, it is critically important that these opinions are seen as substantively impacting the final standard. All the procedures that are established for effective communication with outside parties will enhance public acceptance of the policy board.

Unsolicited views that are important to the policy-making process include the business community's customs and norms in external financial reporting. These values must be explicitly considered if opposition to the directive is to be avoided. In formulating disclosure requirements, policy makers should anticipate resistance to standards that limit management's flexibility to choose accounting procedures. Concern with minimizing bookkeeping costs causes management to favor standards with few operational or implementation complexities. Cognizant of their legal liability for external financial reports, corporations also prefer methods that are objective and result in conservative disclosures.

Inputs to this stage of the model are the factors which influence management's reaction to proposed accounting changes. In addition to general forces within the individual and social system that impede the change process, characteristics specific to the innovation also influence the views of outsiders which must be considered. These intrinsic aspects are determined by the perceptions of the business community regarding the attributes of the proposed standard.

Included in the innovation-specific factors is the expectation of benefits from the adoption of the innovation, which determines the relative advantages from the change. These benefits relate to the tax, regulatory, and political factors; the cost of compliance; and the use of the information by third parties. Such factors potentially impact the corporation's equity market, thereby affecting the economic welfare of both the firm and management. Management's value schemes are again relevant, determining the compatibility or perceived consistency of the specific change with values, norms, past experiences, attitudes, and needs. Complexity in use will influence the reactions to proposed standards. Greater difficulty in understanding the directive and implementing the change enhances negative reactions due to operational factors. A proposed change that allows for partial or gradual implementation, and is thus highly divisible, usually encourages corporate acceptance. And finally, if the expected benefits are significantly visible to management, support for the innovation is more apt to be forthcoming.

While communication aspects were important to insuring management's views entered the policy-making process, the output-oriented channels used to transmit the proposed change also affect the perception of the innovation. Normal communication of directives enhances compatibility with expectations and experiences. Clarity in stating the requirements lessens the perception of complexity.

A final factor influencing the views of outsiders regarding a proposed change involves social system effects, such as the influence of industry leaders or opinion molders within the business community. These parties may actually become the major communication link between the policy board and its constituents.

The fourth element in the policy-making model, assessment of the potential consequences from issuing the directive, follows from the consideration of outside opinions regarding the change. A priori analysis of possible results from an accounting policy involves predicting the short- and long-run effects of a standard. Political and social consequences emanate from the costs and benefits to all affected parties of a change in disclosure practices, ultimately resulting in alterations in resource allocation and wealth distribution. Close consideration should be given to potential behavioral reactions by both information users and suppliers. Once the anticipated consequences are identified, their overall desirability must be assessed in conjunction with social goals. Ex ante impact analysis enables policy makers to anticipate corporate reaction to the directive, and either modify the requirements or devise counterattacks.

An output from this stage is a decision regarding the strategy to be used by the policy maker to engineer a change. The appropriate strategy is influenced by corporate management's felt need for a change, the power position of the policy board and its acceptance as a change agent, the business community's views toward the change and its value scheme in external financial reporting, expected consequences from issuing the directive, attitudinal and/or behavioral conformity desired, and visibility of deviant actions.

A persuasion strategy stresses compatibility with existing norms, and seeks to demonstrate the desirability and beneficial aspects of the change. This is a somewhat weak strategy, relying on positive factors of the particular standard for its effectiveness: agreement on the need for change, acceptance of the policy maker's authority, favorable reactions by the business community, compatibility with existing attitudes, and low potential for dysfunctional consequences.

Relying on education to foster the acceptance of change involves attempts to modify management's beliefs, attitudes, and values. This strategy is most effective if opposition to the innovation is not intense or widespread. Experimentation and informational programs may be used to alter the business community's predispositions and enhance gradual inculcation of the change.

A coercive strategy involves the use of punishments and rewards for behavioral compliance, and it is a feasible approach only when a sufficient power base exists. Management's attitudes are of secondary importance. As with the education strategy, however, less opposition arises if the innovation is compatible with existing values, and policy setters remain sensitive to outside views and potential consequences. Acceptance of the mandate may be enhanced if a period of education and experimentation precedes the use of coercion.

At this point in the paradigm, the policy board is in a position to issue the standard. The policy-making process does not cease with the promulgation of a directive. It is critical that formal procedures be developed to monitor the results from the policy. This ex post consequence analysis includes reactions by information users and suppliers, as well as the impact on resource allocation and wealth distribution patterns. Direct input from those affected by the change includes feedback on their reactions and experiences. The policy board must also establish procedures to monitor consequences independent of such direct responses, as by encouraging empirical research on the impact of a standard.

One input to the ex post consequence analysis is management's reaction to a policy as evidenced by its compliance with the directive. This reaction can be viewed as an innovation decision, involving acceptance or rejection of an FASB standard, and support or opposition to an SEC mandate. Two levels of compliance are important: behavioral conformity and attitudinal acceptance. Behavioral compliance, or overt change in financial reporting practices, is determined by the nature of the policy, the strength of the standard setter's power, and the range over which that power is effective. Changed behavior is most easily secured through the use of coercion, wherein management is highly dependent on the policy maker and the sanctions for noncompliance are severe.

In monitoring the results of a directive, however, the policy setter should be wary of viewing behavioral compliance as indicating success of the policy. Attitudinal acceptance, or covert approval of the innovation, is necessary for long-run maintenance of the change. In a noncoercive situation, this receptiveness is a precondition to adoption of the innovation. Opposition to coerced innovations can be lessened when attitudinal compatibility exists. Covert acceptance is determined in monitoring programs which focus on management's understanding of the innovation, implementation experiences, and modifications in predispositions and values. Ex post consequence analyses should identify the existence of innovation dissonance, or a discrepancy between attitudes and behavior. This condition signals low covert approval of a change, and may explain lack of behavioral conformity with a noncoercive policy.

Management's method of expressing opposition to a policy is an important facet of the ex post consequence analysis. Criticism of the innovation itself may result in undermining the effectiveness and utility of the policy. Challenges to the policy maker may lower overall respect for and authority of that group as a change agent. Thus the consequences from issuing a standard can extend beyond the specific area of financial reporting addressed by the policy.

As a result of its monitoring activities, the policy board must decide whether the standard will be left intact, modified, or revoked. By studying adoption of the innovation over time, lack of success in gaining acceptance of the change will be indicated. The time element is important, as management's experience with an innovation may demonstrate benefits from the change and few implementation problems, thus diminishing resistance to the policy. The monitoring program should allow sufficient time for these reactions to materialize. While it is important that policy setters remain open minded during the course of monitoring consequences, it is even more critical that the business community believe the ex post analysis will have a real impact on the policy-making process. This latter factor is important to the long-run credibility of the standard setter.

The results of monitoring activities determine the outside views and values that must be addressed in reconsidering the directive. The modified policy is scrutinized within the context of the factors of an innovation which influence management's reaction. The potential consequences are weighed, and a strategy for effecting the modifications is adopted. Following promulgation of the amendment or repeal of the standard, the results are monitored with particular attention given to management's compliance activities. This process continues until the policy maker's ultimate objective is attained—formulation of a highly stable policy such that corporate compliance in the absence of influence from the policy setter is ensured. The continuation of innovation dissonance following modification of a directive, such that attitudinal acceptance is not forthcoming, indicates the need to consider revoking the standard.

IMPLICATIONS OF THE MODEL

The accounting policy-making process has been in an evolutionary state since the APB recognized in the early 1960s that it could not rely on persuasion and normative correctness to gain acceptance to its standards by the business community. However, explicit incorporation into the standard-setting mechanism of the many socio-political factors which impinge on the process has been incomplete. Critical areas in need of improvement to broaden the approach to policy making by the FASB and SEC can be identified in conjunction with the model developed in Figure 1-1. The model also holds implications to the CPA profession as it interfaces with the business community, and to corporate management as its role in the process is enhanced. Additionally, future directions for the development of theory and research are revealed.

Accounting policy makers

In considering the overall policy-making process, it is crucial that both the FASB and SEC explicitly recognize the widespread impact of their directives. Policy makers must realize that many parties with vested interests will be affected by and respond to accounting standards, including both users and suppliers of financial reports. It is important that policy boards recognize and admit the consequences of their decisions. This awareness implies a broader, socio-political approach to the formulation of policy. The role of corporate management in the process can no longer be denied. Financial reporting standards affect the welfare of management and the entity, and the corporate community will press its interests on policy makers. Effective standard setting necessitates incorporation of these reactions in a proposed change.

Additionally, since it depends on a legitimate power position, the FASB must realize the importance of the policy-making process to ultimate compliance with its directives. To enhance the acceptance of its standards, the FASB's constituents must perceive the process as equitable. While a well-established approach to standard setting in the private sector does exist, it is important that the mechanism be accepted by the corporate community.

In contrast to the private sector, since the SEC possesses coercive power, the policy-making process is not as critical to acceptance of its rules. The SEC's approach is important, however, to its long-run credibility as a change agent, and to forestall challenges to its viability. Lacking a formal rule-making process, the SEC is seriously vulnerable to attacks on the arbitrary nature of its standard-setting activities. A draft of a proposed rule is always circulated for comment prior to its enactment, and, for major disclosure requirements, the SEC will variantly issue concept releases and hold public hearings. Much of its requirements, however, are formulated using ad hoc, indirect procedures. It is critical that the SEC formalize its entire approach to developing all its accounting directives. While the nature of the requirement could determine the process, the steps to be followed in any given situation should be explicitly stipulated. Formalization of the process would significantly enhance public confidence in the decisions of the SEC, and indicate to the business community what actions it can expect.

Within a model itself, areas that require strengthening by the FASB and SEC can be discerned. When identifying deficiencies in the financial reporting practices of firms needing change, it is critical that both policy boards guard against overstressing the importance of the financial statement user. Dominance of public interest orientations in the formulation of policy gives rise to objectives that focus on the needs of information receivers. This narrow approach encourages neglect of the many varied interests affected by financial reporting standards. As a result, the policy board may suffer a loss of credibility, and attempts to thwart the objectives of a given policy may arise.

Explicitly stating the objectives to be pursued in resolving accounting issues fosters consistency in the process of identifying needed changes. Credibility of the policy maker is enhanced, and compromises to the interests of other parties are better understood. Because the FASB has issued a statement on the objectives of financial reporting, and maintains it intends to pursue these objectives through its policy, innovations suggested by the FASB can be more readily anticipated. The SEC has rejected the need for stipulating the objective of its activities. This stance should be reconsidered by the SEC, since explicit formulation of a purpose to its directives would enhance the perception of consistency in its overall financial-reporting philosophy.

In establishing the acceptance of policy makers as change agents, both the FASB and SEC must realize that their positions of authority are affected by their sensitivity to the broad, socio-political aspects of their decisions. The power bases of the standard-setting bodies, both individually and in relation to each other, influence their acceptance. Because the FASB lacks coercive power, strengthening its authority is critical to its legitimacy. The perception of power can be enhanced, for example, through backing from a higher authority, stronger surveillance programs, and increased sanctions for noncompliance with its requirements. With a weak power position, attitudinal acceptance of FASB policies becomes more important.

On the contrary, the SEC possesses sufficient power to ensure enforcement of its directives. It must be careful not to misuse coercion by forcing compliance with directives in areas where the business community questions its sanctioned right. The SEC should recognize that its authority depends on the relationship between its legitimacy and coercive power. Establishing disclosure requirements outside of its effective range may hinder attitudinal acceptance of its policy, hurt its credibility, and instill resistance to its power and the specific directive.

Critical to the acceptance of both policy boards is the proper juxtaposition of their relative power such that they do not appear adversaries. While it may not be necessary that spheres of responsibility be delineated (e.g., measurement versus reporting issues), it is crucial that they coordinate their activities and remain highly sensitive to each other's actions. At all costs, they must avoid clashes, power struggles, conflicting policies, and usurpation of authority. While it is important to the FASB's authority that the SEC support its policy actions, the SEC must realize that its credibility is also influenced by the existence of conflicts.

The future for progress in this area is somewhat dimmed by the SEC's active oversight role of the policy-making activities in the private sector. In a speech regarding the FASB's inflation accounting proposal, SEC Chairman Harold M. Williams stated the efficacy of the FASB in dealing with controversial issues is at a critical juncture. Factors cited as important to the viability of the FASB centered on the effectiveness of its standard-setting process as determined by issuance of timely standards responsive to needed changes, active innovation and experimentation, and leadership rather than consensus building in formulating policy. Williams was explicit regarding the possibility of SEC intervention if the FASB appears inactive:

> While the private sector has demonstrated the ability—often slow and reluctant—to be responsive on accounting matters, it has done so largely in reaction to external prodding. In my judgment, it is essential that this pattern change. . . . While the Commission will consider amending or rescinding ASR 190, if an acceptable final [FASB] statement is adopted, we would not look positively at the loss of another year (FASB 1979e, pp. 69, 76).

The stage in the policy-making model wherein outside views are explicitly incorporated and management's values are considered in the formulation of the directive, is often omitted by policy setters. Management's reactions are criticized as unfounded and irrational, and inclusion of the corporate community in the process is judged inappropriate. Both the FASB and SEC should cease this surface rejection of the role of management and look deeper into the motivation for its reactions to standards. For any given policy, identification of affected parties, vested interests, and social system effects should occur early. The attributes of a specific innovation should be scrutinized, with full realization that these characteristics, as perceived from the vantage of the self-interests of an affected party, will influence the success of the policy. Realistically, subordination of these self-interests to the public good cannot be expected. Management's financial-reporting norms indicate potential aversion to standards which, for example, reduce flexibility or lessen objectivity. Serious consideration should be given to modifying a suggested change to overcome its dysfunctional aspects.

While outside views must be considered even if they are not a part of direct communication from affected parties, formal channels should be established for the incorporation of such views into the policy-making process. Lacking a structured procedure for creating its financial reporting standards, the SEC is seriously deficient in its provision for feedback. Limited avenues for such input do exist: occasional concept releases, public hearings, and proposed rulings exposed for comment. As a part of the formalization of its overall policy-making process, the SEC should structure communication channels to facilitate the solicitation of outside views. Sensitivity to varied interests is restricted further by the dominance of lawyers as Commissioners. Broader representation among those making decisions regarding accounting issues would strengthen the role of affected parties.

Concerned with the need to establish credibility and enhance its authority position, the FASB has well-established procedures for incorporating outside views. Representation at all decision-making levels has been broadened to include a wide range of parties interested in the formulation of accounting policy. The public is kept informed on the activities of the FASB, and several opportunities exist for interested parties to respond at various stages in the policy-making process. Critical to the FASB is ensuring valid input has a real impact on the final directive. The formalization of communication channels will be a fruitless gesture if substantive modification in the policy does not materialize.

Both the FASB and SEC have endorsed the need for ex ante consequence analyses. They have also, however, deemphasized the real impact such considerations should have, and they have failed to explicitly formulate a means by which such considerations can enter the decision-making process. Formal programs should be devised for considering the potential consequences of all proposed standards. This first involves the difficult process of developing procedures for predicting the short- and long-run impact on all parties potentially affected; that is, the costs and benefits of a policy. Next, the overall desirability of the effects must be assessed, requiring policy makers to explicitly formulate economic and social objectives.

The potential consequences and the policy maker's power position influence the selection of a strategy to enact change. For the FASB, persuasion has proven ineffective due to its weak power position, and coercion is impossible without direct backing by the SEC or Congress. The use of persuasion by the SEC is precluded by its coercive power base. Both the FASB and SEC should carefully consider the use of an education strategy, including in those situations where coercion is seen by the SEC as eventually needed. Education is particularly important in the accounting environment, since attitudinal acceptance plays an important role in gaining support of policy directives. By demonstrating the positive factors of an innovation, an education strategy encompassing experimentation can overcome resistance to proposed changes.

Monitoring the results of an enacted policy is facilitated by formalized procedures. While the SEC has concurred with the desirability for ex post consequence analyses, and has informally agreed to monitor the impact of major new disclosure requirements, it has also cited limited resources for such activities and uncertainty as to the appropriate procedures. A critical aspect to maintaining the credibility of the SEC, and a part of the formalization of its policy-making process, involves the development of monitoring procedures to be followed in all its policy activities. The FASB has devised such programs through its postenactment reviews, support of research, and formalized means for request by outsiders for review of specific standards. Critical to the FASB is ensuring that the results of its monitoring activities have a substantive impact on the policy-making process. The FASB must accordingly remain open to timely modification or repeal of a standard when it appears appropriate.

Corporate compliance with directives is an important aspect of ex post consequence analysis. The critical role of attitudinal acceptance cannot be overemphasized. Management's covert state is a precondition to adoption of innovations in optional or collective decisions, and lessens resistance to authority decisions. In all cases, compatibility between management's values and overt actions is necessary for long-run acceptance of the change. The SEC in particular must recognize that the behavioral conformity which results from a coerced innovation does not represent "success" of the policy.

Lacking attitudinal acceptance, an accounting policy may invite severe corporate opposition. The FASB and SEC must explicitly assess the tangible and intangible costs of this situation. While the expenses related to constant surveillance can be identified, costs also arise from criticisms of the innovation which undermine the effectiveness of the change and challenges to the policy board which threaten its authority and power. Such opposition weakens the chances of successful implementation of the change, including both behavioral and attitudinal acceptance. Carefully monitoring these reactions over time will reveal if the resistance is temporary or permanent, and indicate the need for modification of the policy.

The CPA profession

As members of the accounting profession, CPAs are an important part of the standard-setting mechanism. To the extent they influence the policy maker's deliberations, they should be aware of the process for effecting change and work within the framework developed in Figure 1-1. The model indicates the critical role of the CPA profession: to act as mediators between the accounting policy maker and corporate management. In this role, CPAs can facilitate change at each stage of the process.

In addition to alerting the policy maker to deficiencies in reporting practices needing change, including those which arise from current financial accounting standards, the auditing profession can help demonstrate the need for proposed changes to its corporate clients. The power of policy makers, especially the FASB, is greatly enhanced by support for its directives from CPAs. The policy-making model implies this sanction is critical, as secured through requirements by individual CPAs that firms comply with standards and general acceptance by auditors collectively of the authority of policy makers.

Auditors act as an important communication source in the process of formulating accounting standards. This implies that CPAs should attempt to inform management of proposed and enacted policies as well as provide feedback to policy makers regarding outside views of directives. They must realize their role is important input to the standard setter in discerning the real impact of a proposed rule on the business community and assessing the potential consequences from its issuance.

The strategy used to enact a reporting requirement determines the appropriate role of the CPA. If persuasion is used, auditors can facilitate the change process by demonstrating the compatibility of the standard with management's values. CPAs should be aware of their critical function in an education strategy. By dealing directly with the corporate community, CPAs can effectively explain the requirements and encourage experimentation and innovation, thereby influencing management's attitudes. In a coercive situation, the auditor should attempt to lessen resistance and opposition by identifying the most troublesome aspects of the directive and helping management overcome them.

Firsthand experience with the operational aspects of an accounting standard establishes CPAs as central in ex post monitoring activities. Here again, the auditing profession should realize its important role as a communication link. In this context, attempts should be made to conduct analyses of the impact of a standard enabling policy makers to discern real consequences from alleged effects. The CPA also functions as an important forewarner to the standard setter on the existence of corporate opposition with potentially detrimental effects to the standard itself and the policy setter. Auditors will be among the first to be able to determine if attitudinal acceptance of a policy is forthcoming. They should accordingly keep policy makers alerted as to the need for modification or repeal of a standard.

In addition to enabling CPAs to facilitate the process of change the policy-making model helps the auditing profession understand it relationship vis-à-vis corporate management. Specification of management's value schemes in financial reporting, and the factors of a proposed change which influence its reactions, fosters an understanding of the pressures which will be applied on CPAs. By anticipating these responses, individual auditors can more effectively deal with conflict situations, perhaps enhancing the perception of their independence from the desires of corporate clients.

Corporate management

A formalized policy-making process establishes a means for the business community to responsibly enter standard-setting activities. At every stage of the model, the business community has an opportunity to provide input to the deliberations and potentially affect the output. Such input may occur individually as through corporate management, or collectively as through industry trade groups or professional organizations such as the FEI. In all cases, the business community must remember that its interactions with policy makers should be responsible and professional. The nature of the interaction is crucial for corporate management to maintain credibility, and become an effective part of the policy-making process.

Coerced and unwanted changes may be forestalled by the business community if it takes the initiative in identifying areas of deficiencies and suggesting remedies. Management should resist the natural tendency to support the status quo, and be more open to voluntary and self-initiated innovation and experimentation.

Long-run viability of the policy-making process hinges upon corporate acceptance of current policy boards. The business community should give careful consideration to the eventual outcome of repeated attacks on a standard setter's authority. This is especially true for the FASB, which depends on broad-based acceptance for its legitimate power position. Severe criticism of the FASB could result in the formulation of a government standard-setting body with coercive power. In lodging attacks on the authority of the private-sector policy board, the corporate community should seriously consider the desirability of this alternative. If deemed unpalatable, corporate management should make short-term compromises in its opposition to specific accounting standards to mitigate the perception of ineffectiveness by the FASB and avoid the possibility of mandated uniformity for all reporting practices.

In communicating its position on proposed standards to policy makers, management can facilitate the process and ensure attenuation to its views by using normal communication channels. It should not expect that exposing its views through the financial press, for example, will be an effective means for impacting a policy. Additionally, real attitudes and values should be revealed to standard setters. Opposing changes in financial reporting practices because they represent deviations from the traditional historical-cost accounting model is often a surface objection. Management should admit its motivations are usually more directly related to its self-interests, such as the impact on compensation, equity markets, and potential regulation. The business community's credibility within the standard-setting process, and possibly the impact of its views, will be enhanced by indepth analysis and communication of the real factors motivating its reactions to proposed standards. Analogously, management should carefully assess expected consequences from a policy and avoid automatic opposition merely because it represents a change.

Once the policy has been formulated and the standard setter has adopted a strategy, corporate management should give serious consideration to the long-term implications of its reactions. While the business community may resist adopting an innovation, management should take seriously programs of persuasion and education adopted by policy makers. Honest attempts to incorporate a change will provide important feedback to the change agent, and perhaps forestall the use of a stronger strategy such as coercion or appeal for sanction to policy boards with higher authority.

In the process of monitoring results, management can play an important role by facilitating research on the real impact of a reporting requirement. The corporate community is responsible for effectively communicating its experiences to policy makers. And in the process of compliance, management should again remain sensitive to the long-run impact of its opposition on the private-sector standard-setting mechanism. Making a sham of reporting requirements by discrediting their utility or finding loopholes to avoid compliance, or challenging the credibility of policy makers, seriously damages the authority of the policy board. Management should give the feedback mechanism a chance to work, and allow for modifications in reporting requirements, before it embarks on campaigns to undermine the standard-setting function.

Accounting theory and research

Implications to accounting theory of the socio-political approach to formulating policy center on two areas: (1) the weakness of normative orientations in general, and (2) the limited role of theory in resolving controversial issues.

The development of a framework that incorporates the many influencing factors in the policy-making process reveals defects in relying on theoretical solutions to accounting controversies. Identification of the sociological aspects of disclosure requirements indicates that formulating standards in pursuit of economic reality detracts from their acceptance. Management does not establish its reporting practices based on a mythical true measurement of reality, nor does it respond to accounting standards from this vantage.

The behavioral aspects of accounting measurement, including reactions from both financial statement users and preparers, can no longer be ignored. Myopic concentration on the user, however, is also seen as deficient within the context of the policy-setting model. The user is an important input to establishing the need for policy and assessing the ex ante and ex post consequences of a standard. Submitting disclosure requirements to user-oriented criteria such as relevance and reliability leads to neglect of the factors which foster corporate reaction to a standard. The third theoretical approach to policy setting, the supplier orientation, is potentially useful to developing a realistic framework for creating disclosure requirements. The major weakness of this orientation is its relative immaturity. Much progress must be made in extending agency theory to the corporate-reporting system, and integrating sociological and political factors in the theory.

The weaknesses of the major theoretical approaches used for resolving accounting issues are responsible for their limited role in effectively developing reporting requirements. Policy makers, the CPA profession, and corporate management have all used the theoretical argument most consistent with their preferred solution to an issue. Depending on the orientation chosen, any of a number of resolutions to a given problem emerge as viable. The policy-making model developed in Figure 1-1 reveals the many factors which enter the process. The critical implication is that no one theoretical approach to resolving accounting issues will emerge as able to handle all the interacting variables and consistently provide acceptable solutions in all instances. It is inconceivable that agreement could ever be reached on a paradigm considered adequate for dealing with the many vested interests of affected parties. Endeavors by policy makers and theoreticians to develop such a paradigm appear futile.

Implications to accounting research of the policy-making model emerge from the limited contribution of theory to the formulation of accounting standards. The most critical need is for descriptive studies of the entire policy-setting environment. This implies positive research in two areas: (1) observing the events that occur in formulating reporting requirements, and (2) identifying the reasons for the emergence of such events. For example, research should focus on identifying when various social systems become involved in policy making, and then seek to explain the motivation for their involvement. Analogously, positive research would first observe when the implementation aspect of a reporting requirement is important to management, and next identify why operationalization is critical in that particular situation.

The prescription for expanded descriptive research is not limited to focusing on the business community's role in financial reporting. While the economic reality and user orientations were criticized for their normative focus, reexamination of these orientations from a descriptive vantage could reveal their relevance to the standard-setting function. Observations of when measurement and disclosure of current value materially affects the firm's financial statements could help identify those factors which give rise to a substantive impact. This situation would indicate when economic reality considerations become relevant to establishing the need for changes in reporting practices. Focusing on when specific disclosures impact the decisions of users, and then studying why there is a change in this behavior, provides important input to the ex post consequences of disclosure requirements.

Within the policy-making model itself, positive research is needed at all stages of the process. Observation of situations where policy making was initiated would indicate how serious deficiencies need to become for standard setters to intercede. Actions by the business community to enact changes can be scrutinized to determine what level of voluntary activities is sufficient to forestall the standard-setting process. The pressure applied by outside parties on policy boards can be studied to discern which are most influential in prompting action. Specific interest groups resisting an innovation can be identified, and the causes for low perceptions of the need for change sought. Identification should be made of the conditions of the environment which are most functional to instilling the need for change within management.

Focusing on previous policy-making situations, the interaction between the standard setter's power position and its acceptance level can be studied, revealing which power bases are most successful for enhancing the change process. The influence of the policy maker's power position on the appropriate strategy is also relevant. By studying issues such as the investment tax credit, oil and gas accounting, and inflation accounting, insight can be gained into the effect of power relationships between two policy boards on the standard-setting process, and the impact of confrontations and power struggles.

Management's involvement in the policy-making process should be studied by determining what conditions prevail to encourage its active participation in the resolution of controversial issues, as well as the nature of its involvement. Focusing on past and present communication channels should reveal which avenues are most effective for the business community to express its views. The predominance of specific values can be correlated with the acceptance or rejection of a given standard. Indepth research needs to be conducted into the real incentives and factors that influence management's reactions, including the situations which give rise to perceptions of dysfunctional consequences. Extension of previous research on the positive theory of relative advantages would indicate if this is an accurate description of the factors determining economic benefits. Beyond economic factors, studying specific change situations should reveal which behavioral factors influence the perception of the innovation's attributes. This will enable description of the entire change environment encompassing social system effects, social structure, cultural values, communication channels, and other sociological aspects. Additionally, the relative importance of compatibility, complexity, and trialability may be indicated.

As policy setters modify their processes, identification can be made of the factors most critical in assessing potential consequences. The proper role of cost/benefit analyses in finalizing reporting standards should emerge. Experimentation with measuring benefits and identifying the real costs of disclosure requirements is critical to effectively conducting a priori consequence analyses. Consideration should be given to the entire change situation surrounding specific policies, including the change agent's power base and the nature of the innovation, to determine what types of strategies are most functional.

Following the issuance of a standard, identification should be made of the factors that are present when corporate acceptance of an innovation results. Characteristics of the change environment should be corresponded to the various types of responses which emerge. The nature of compliance can be related to the parties involved, power positions, characteristics of the innovation, and strategies employed. In situations where management has appealed to higher authorities, the conditions that prevailed should be specified.

Descriptive research questions can be narrowed further to focus specifically on the areas of the processes followed by the FASB and SEC most in need of attention. Inquiry should be made into the reasons why policy makers resist recognizing and accepting the economic consequences of their activities, and ways to increase their sensitivity to these issues should be found. For a variety of enacted standards, the interaction between the FASB's policy-making process and the acceptance of its policy statements should be scrutinized to facilitate improvements in its procedures. Because the SEC needs to formalize its process, the past effectiveness of alternative procedures must be considered in structuring its approach.

Looking at the objectives and consequences of enacted policies would reveal the effect of overemphasis on the role of the financial statement user in identifying needed changes in the corporate disclosure system. Previous policy-making situations may indicate how the FASB's authority can be strengthened, as well as the effect from extending the SEC's power beyond its effective range. Situations where both the FASB and SEC have been functionally involved, such as lease accounting, provide insight as to how power clashes can be avoided. Corporate reaction to policies indicates the most effective means for the FASB to substantively incorporate outside views in its policies. Studying the FASB's procedures might enable the SEC to establish formal systems of representation and communication channels for soliciting outside views in its deliberations.

Experiences in the development of ex ante consequence analyses will indicate formal procedures that should be instituted into the policy-making process. Numerous policy situations can be studied to determine when an education strategy is most effective and how it should be used. Close scrutiny of current FASB post-enactment activities will determine how the results from monitoring programs can substantively impact the FASB's standards. The FASB's experiences will also indicate those aspects that should be formalized in an ex post consequence analysis for the SEC. Studying the success and failure of previously issued standards should reveal the role of attitudinal acceptance in the process of engineering change.

SUMMARY

The chapter began with a reiteration of the need to adopt a sociological perspective to formulating accounting policy. This implies considering the effect of reporting standards on all parties, including corporate management as the information supplier. The factors that influence management's reaction to reporting requirements become relevant, and they are seen to depend on the nature of the policy's impact on the firm.

Consistent with management's natural interest in financial disclosures, a model was developed to incorporate the important elements into a policy-making process. The mechanism begins with the identification of the need for change and the suggestion of an innovation by the policy maker. Acceptance of the standard setter as an authorized change agent is also crucial, with the policy maker's power base an important input to this consideration. Outside views and management's values must be assessed, and the factors influencing reactions to standards become relevant. Assessment of potential consequences indicates the appropriate strategy to be adopted. Issuance of the policy is followed by a program to monitor the results, with management's compliance an input to the consequence analysis. The results from the process reveal needed modification or repeal of the standard, and the policy-making activities continue accordingly.

This framework was used to identify areas where current policy-making procedures are deficient. The appropriate role of the CPA profession and corporate management was also revealed by the structure of the process. Weaknesses of theoretical approaches to resolving issues emerge, and the role of theory is restricted by its use to support self-interests. The greatest research need is to gain an understanding of the realities of the standard-setting environment through descriptive and positive study.

References

Adams, Don. "The Monkey and the Fish: Cultural Pitfalls of an Educational Advisor." *International Development Review* 2 (1960): 22–24.

Advisory Committee on Corporate Disclosure. *Report of the Advisory Committee on Corporate Disclosure to the Securities and Exchange Commission.* Washington, D.C.: U.S. Government Printing Office, 1977.

American Institute of Certified Public Accountants. *Experimental Program Financial Accounting Models.* New York: AICPA, April 1977.

American Institute of Certified Public Accountants. *Code of Professional Ethics.* New York: AICPA, 1972.

Armstrong, Marshall. "The Politics of Establishing Accounting Standards." *Journal of Accountancy* (February 1977): 76–79.

"Arthur Andersen Sues SEC." *Journal of Accountancy* (September 1976): 7–8.

Arthur Young & Company. *Disclosing Replacement-Cost Data.* New York: Arthur Young & Company, 1977.

Asebrook, Richard J., and Carmichael, D. R. "Reporting on Forecasts: A Survey of Attitudes." *Journal of Accountancy* (August 1973): 38–48.

Bastable, C. W. "Is SEC Replacement Cost Data Worth the Effort?" *Journal of Accountancy* (October 1977): 68–76.

Beaver, William H. "What Should Be the FASB's Objectives?" *Journal of Accountancy* (August 1973): 49–56.

Buckley, John W. "The FASB and Impact Analysis." *Management Accounting* (April 1976): 13–17.

Burton, John C. "Paper Shuffling and Economic Reality." *Journal of Accountancy* (January 1973a): 20, 26, 28.

Burton, John C. "Some General and Specific Thoughts on the Accounting Environment." *Journal of Accountancy* (October 1973b): 40–46.

Carlson, Arthur. "ASR 190—The Grand Experiment." *Management Accounting* (October 1977): 23–25.

Carmichael, D. R. "The Implications for Accounting Practice of the FASB's New Approach." *Journal of Accountancy* (May 1979): 76-84.

Carpenter, Charles G., and Daily, R. Austin. "Controllers and CPAs: Two Views of Published Forecasts." *Business Horizons* (August 1974): 73-78.

Chandra, Gyan, and Greenball, Melvin N. "Management Reluctance to Disclose: An Empirical Study." *Abacus* (Winter 1977): 141-154.

Chatov, Robert. *Corporate Financial Reporting: Public or Private Control?* New York: The Free Press, 1975.

Chin, Robert, and Benne, Kenneth. "General Strategies for Effecting Changes in Human Systems." In *Creating Social Change,* edited by Gerald Zaltman, Philip Kotler, Ira Kaufman. New York: Holt, Rinehart and Winston, 1972, pp. 233-254.

Comiskey, Eugene E., and Groves, R. E. "The Adoption and Diffusion of an Accounting Innovation." *Accounting and Business Research* (Winter 1972): 67-77.

Committee on Concepts and Standards for External Financial Reports. *Statement on Accounting Theory and Theory Acceptance.* Sarasota, Florida: American Accounting Association, 1977.

Cooper, Kerry; Flory, Steven; and Grossman, Steven. "New Ballgame for Oil and Gas Accounting." *CPA Journal* (January 1979): 11-17.

Copeland, Ronald M., and Shank, John K. "LIFO and the Diffusion of Innovation." *Empirical Research in Accounting: Selected Studies, 1971.* Supplement to *Journal of Accounting Research* (1971): 196-224.

Corbin, D. A. "SEC Replacement Costs: Suggestions for Full Disclosure." *Management Accounting* (August 1977): 11-18.

"Corporations Doubt Usefulness of Replacement Cost Data, Survey Shows." *Management Accounting* (August 1976): 5-6.

Defliese, Philip L. Professor, Graduate School of Business, Columbia University, letter dated September 7, 1979.

DeWelt, R. L. "Replacement Cost—Another Nightmare for Accountants." *Management Accounting* (October 1977): 17-22.

Dukes, Ronald E. *An Empirical Investigation of the Effects of Statement of Financial Accounting Standards No. 8 on Security Return Behavior.* Stamford, Conn.: FASB, 1978.

Dyckman, Thomas R.; Downes, David H.; and Magee, Robert P. *Efficient Capital Markets and Accounting: A Critical Analysis.* Englewood Cliffs, N.J.: Prentice-Hall, Inc., 1975.

"Enticing Companies Out on the Forecasting Limb." *Business Week* (February 12, 1979): 96.

Evans, Thomas G.; Folks, William R., Jr.; and Jilling, Michael. *The Impact of Statement of Financial Accounting Standards No. 8 on the Foreign Exchange Risk Management Practices of American Multinationals: An Economic Impact Study.* Stamford, Conn.: FASB, 1978.

Financial Accounting Foundation, Financial Accounting Standards Board. *Annual Reports 1977.* Stamford, Conn.: FASB, 1978.

Financial Accounting Foundation Structure Committee. *Structure of Establishing Financial Accounting Standards.* Stamford, Conn.: FASB, 1977.

Financial Accounting Standards Board. "SEC Meets with Standards Board." *Status Report.* Stamford, Conn.: FASB, February 9, 1979a.

Financial Accounting Standards Board. *Qualitative Characteristics: Criteria for Selecting and Evaluating Financial Accounting and Reporting Practices.* Exposure Draft. Stamford, Conn.: FASB, August 9, 1979b.

Financial Accounting Standards Board. "FASB Chairman Testifies at Senator Eagleton's Subcommittee Hearings." *Status Report.* Stamford, Conn.: FASB, August 24, 1979c.

Financial Accounting Standards Board. *Financial Reporting and Changing Prices.* Statement of Financial Accounting Standards No. 33. Stamford, Conn.: FASB, September 1979d.

Financial Accounting Standards Board. *Financial Accounting and Changing Prices: The Conference.* Stamford, Conn.: FASB, 1979e.

Financial Accounting Standards Board. "Summary of Changes Made as a Result of Structure Committee Recommendations." *Status Report.* Stamford, Conn.: FASB, June 21, 1978a.

Financial Accounting Standards Board. "Statement by Trustees Supports FASB on Oil and Gas Accounting." *Status Report.* Stamford, Conn.: FASB, September 29, 1978b.

Financial Accounting Standards Board. *Accounting for Certain Service Transactions.* Invitation to Comment. Stamford, Conn.: FASB, October 23, 1978c.

Financial Accounting Standards Board. *Objectives of Financial Reporting by Business Enterprises.* Statement of Financial Accounting Concepts No. 1. Stamford, Conn.: FASB, November 1978d.

Financial Accounting Standards Board. *Financial Reporting and Changing Prices.* Exposure Draft. Stamford, Conn.: FASB, December 1978e.

Financial Accounting Standards Board. *Rules of Procedure Amended and Restated.* Stamford, Conn.: FASB, 1978f.

Flamholtz, Eric, and Cook, Ellen. "Connotative Meaning and its Role in Accounting Change: A Field Study." *Accounting, Organization and Society* 3 no. 2 (1978): 115–139.

Foster, George. *Financial Statement Analysis.* Englewood Cliffs, N.J.: Prentice-Hall, Inc. 1978.

French, J. R. P., Jr., and Raven, Bertram. "The Bases of Social Power." In *Group Dynamics,* edited by D. Cartwright and A. Zander. Evanston, Ill.: Row, Peterson, 1960, pp. 607–623.

Gagnon, J. M. "The Purchase-Pooling Choice: Some Empirical Evidence." *Journal of Accounting Research* (Spring 1971): 52–72.

Garsombke, H. Perrin. "ASR 190: Implementation, Costs and Benefits." *CPA Journal* (February 1978): 23–26.

Gellein, Oscar S. "The Task of the Standard Setter." *Journal of Accountancy* (December 1978): 75–79.

Gerboth, Dale L. "Research, Intuition, and Politics." *Accounting Review* (July 1973): 475-482.

Gerboth, Dale L. " 'Muddling Through' with the APB." *Journal of Accountancy* (May 1972): 42-49.

Goldman, Arien, and Barlev, Benzion. "The Auditor-Firm Conflict of Interests: Its Implications for Independence." *Accounting Review* (October 1974): 707-718.

Golub, Steven J. Professional Accounting Fellow, Securities and Exchange Commission, letter dated January 11, 1979.

Gonedes, Nicholas J., and Dopuch, Nicholas. "Capital Market Equilibrium, Information Production, and Selecting Accounting Techniques: Theoretical Framework and Review of Empirical Work." *Studies on Financial Accounting Objectives: 1974.* Supplement to *Journal of Accounting Research* (1974): 48-129.

Goshay, Robert C. *Statement of Financial Accounting Standards No. 5: Impact on Corporate Risk and Insurance Management.* Stamford, Conn.: FASB, 1978.

Hepworth, S. R. "Smoothing Periodic Income." *Accounting Review* (January 1953): 32-40.

Hicks, James O., Jr. "An Examination of Accounting Interest Groups' Differential Perceptions of Innovation." *Accounting Review* (April 1978): 371-388.

Hornbostel, Charles G. "Financial Challenges in a Changing Regulatory Environment." *Financial Executive* (December 1972): 23-27.

Horngren, Charles T. "Will the FASB Be Here in the 1980s?" *Journal of Accountancy* (November 1976): 90-96.

Horngren, Charles T. "The Marketing of Accounting Standards." *Journal of Accountancy* (October 1973): 61-66.

Horngren, Charles T. "Accounting Principles: Private or Public Sector?" *Journal of Accountancy* (May 1972): 37-41.

Hussein, Mohamed E. A. *A Socio-Political Framework of the Process of Adopting Generally Accepted Accounting Standards.* Unpublished Ph.D. dissertation, University of Pittsburgh, 1977.

Ijiri, Yuji; Jaedicke, Robert; and Knight, Kenneth. "The Effects of Accounting Alternatives on Management Decisions." In *Research in Accounting Measurement,* edited by Robert Jaedicke, Yuji Ijiri, and Oswald Nielsen. Evanston, Ill.: American Accounting Association, 1966, pp. 186-199.

"Inflation Accounting: Nobody Likes the FASB's New Approach—But What Else Is There?" *Business Week* (October 15, 1979): 68-72, 74.

"Inflation Accounting: The FASB Takes the Plunge." *Business Week* (January 22, 1979): 85-86.

Jensen, Michael C. "Reflections on the State of Accounting Research and the Regulation of Accounting." Working Paper Series No. GPB-76-7, Graduate School of Management, The University of Rochester, May 1976.

Jensen, Michael C., and Meckling, William H. "Theory of the Firm: Management Behavior, Agency Costs and Ownership Structure." *Journal of Financial Economics* 3 (1976): 305–360.

Kelly-Newton, Lauren. "A Sociological Investigation of the U.S. Mandate for Replacement Cost Disclosures: A Theoretical and Empirical Analysis." AISRP Working Paper No. 79-11, Graduate School of Management, University of California, Los Angeles, January 1979.

Kirk, Donald J. "How to Keep Politics Out of Standard Setting: Making Private Sector Rule-Making Work." *Journal of Accountancy* (September 1978): 92–94.

Kotler, Philip. "The Elements of Social Action." In *Creating Social Change*, edited by Gerald Zaltman, Philip Kotler, Ira Kaufman. New York: Holt, Rinehart and Winston, 1972, pp. 172–185.

Livingstone, John Leslie. "A Behaviorial Study of Tax Allocation in Electric Utility Regulation." *Accounting Review* (July 1967): 544–552.

"A Major Audit for FASB-8." *Business Week* (January 29, 1978): 102–103.

May, Robert G., and Sundem, Gary L. "Research for Accounting Policy: An Overview." *Accounting Review* (October 1976): 747–763.

Mayer-Sommer, Alan P. "Understanding and Acceptance of the Efficient Markets Hypothesis and its Accounting Implications." *Accounting Review* (January 1979): 88–106.

McLagan, Donald L., and Ross, Jay N. "Replacement Cost Accounting Can Serve Management Too." *Financial Executive* (August 1977): 30–35.

Moonitz, Maurice. *Obtaining Agreement on Standards.* Studies in Accounting Research No. 8. Sarasota, Florida: American Accounting Association, 1974.

Moonitz, Maurice. "Some Reflections on the Investment Credit Experience." *Journal of Accounting Research* (Spring 1966): 47–61.

Murphy, Thomas. "A Businessman's Views on Uniform Standards." *Journal of Accountancy* (May 1979): 86–87.

Nash, Manning. "Discussion of LIFO and the Diffusion of Innovation." *Empirical Research in Accounting: Selected Studies 1971*. Supplement to *Journal of Accounting Research* (1971): 228–230.

Nichols, Donald, and Price, Kenneth. "The Auditor-Firm Conflict: An Analysis Using Concepts of Exchange Theory." *Accounting Review* (April 1976): 335–346.

Peat, Marwick, Mitchell & Company. *A Survey of the Economic Impacts of FASB Statement No. 8, 'Accounting for the Translation of Foreign Currency Transactions and Foreign Currency Financial Statements'* New York: Peat, Marwick, Mitchell & Company, 1977.

Prakash, Prem, and Rappaport, Alfred. "Information Inductance and Its Significance for Accounting." *Accounting, Organizations, and Society* 2, no. 1 (1977): 29–38.

Rappaport, Alfred. "Economic Impact of Accounting Standards—Implications for the FASB." *Journal of Accountancy* (May 1977): 89–98.

"Replacement Costs: Clarification or Confusion?" *Business Week* (August 9, 1976): 54–56.

Rogers, Everett M. "The Change Agency and Change Target." In *Creating Social Change,* edited by Gerald Zaltman, Philip Kotler, and Ira Kaufman. New York: Holt, Rinehart and Winston, 1972, pp. 194–213.

Rogers, Everett M., and Shoemaker, F. Floyd. *Communication of Innovations.* New York: The Free Press, 1971.

Ronen, Joshua; Sadan, Simcha; and Snow, Charles. "Income Smoothing: A Review." *The Accounting Journal* (1977): 11–29.

Rothman, Jack. *Planning and Organizing for Social Change.* New York: Columbia University Press, 1974.

Savoie, Leonard M. "Accounting Attitudes." In *Institutional Issues in Public Accounting,* edited by Robert R. Sterling. Lawrence, Kansas: Scholars Book Co., 1974, pp. 317–327.

"The SEC Rulemaking Process." *CPA Journal* (June 1978): 47–49.

Securities and Exchange Commission. *Preliminary Response of the Commission to the Recommendations of the Advisory Committee on Corporate Disclosure,* Release Nos. 33-5906, 34-14471. Washington, D.C.: U.S. Government Printing Office, February 15, 1978a.

Securities and Exchange Commission. "The Role of the Commission." Excerpt from *The Securities and Exchange Commission Report to Congress on the Accounting Profession and the Commission's Oversight Role.* Washington, D.C.: U.S. Government Printing Office, July 1978b.

Securities and Exchange Commission. *Adoption of Requirements for Financial Accounting and Reporting Practices of Oil and Gas Producing Activities.* Accounting Series Release No. 253. Washington, D.C.: U.S. Government Printing Office, August 31, 1978c.

Securities and Exchange Commission. *Notice of Adoption of Amendments to Regulation S-X Requiring Disclosure of Certain Replacement Cost Data.* Accounting Series Release No. 190. Washington, D.C.: U.S. Government Printing Office, March 23, 1976.

Securities and Exchange Commission. *Statement of Policy on the Establishment and Improvement of Accounting Principles and Standards.* Accounting Series Release No. 150. Washington, D.C.: U.S. Government Printing Office, December 20, 1973.

Securities and Exchange Commission. *Administrative Policy on Financial Statements.* Accounting Series Release No. 4. Washington, D.C.: U.S. Government Printing Office, April 25, 1938.

Shank, John K., and Copeland, Ronald M. "Corporate Personality Theory and Changes in Accounting Methods: An Empirical Test." *Accounting Review* (July 1973): 494–501.

Skousen, K. Fred. "Standards for Reporting by Lines of Business." *Journal of Accountancy* (November 1978): 65–72.

Skousen, K. Fred. *An Introduction to the SEC.* Cincinnati: South-Western Publishing Co., 1976.

Solomons, David. "The Politicization of Accounting." *Journal of Accountancy* (November 1978a): 65-72.

Solomons, David. "Judging Accounting Policies." In *1978 Accounting Research Convocation,* edited by Jonathan Davies. University, Alabama: University of Alabama, 1978b.

Sorter, George H.; Becker, Selwyn W.; Archibald, T. R.; and Beaver, William. "Corporate Personality as Reflected in Accounting Decisions: Some Preliminary Findings." *Journal of Accounting Research* (Autumn 1964): 183-196.

Sterling, Robert R. "Accounting Research, Education and Practice." *Journal of Accountancy* (September 1973): 44-52.

Study Group on the Objectives of Financial Statements. *Objectives of Financial Statements.* New York: American Institute of Certified Public Accountants, 1973.

Study on Establishment of Accounting Principles. *Establishing Financial Accounting Standards.* New York: American Institute of Certified Public Accountants, 1972.

Tritschler, Charles A. "A Sociological Perspective on Accounting Innovation." *The International Journal of Accounting Education and Research* (Spring 1970): 39-67.

U.S. Senate Subcommittee on Reports, Accounting and Management of the Committee on Government Operations. *Improving the Accountability of Publicly Owned Corporations and Their Auditors.* Washington, D.C.: U.S. Government Printing Office, 1977.

U.S. Senate Subcommittee on Reports, Accounting and Management of the Committee on Government Operations. *The Accounting Establishment: A Staff Study.* Washington, D.C.: U.S. Government Printing Office, 1976.

Walton, Richard E. "Two Strategies of Social Change and Their Dilemmas." *Journal of Applied Behavioral Science* (April-June 1965): 167-179.

Warren, Donald I. "Power Visibility and Conformity in Formal Organizations." *American Sociological Review* 33, no. 6 (1968): 951-970.

Watson, Goodwin. "Resistance to Change." In *Concepts for Social Change,* vol. I, edited by Goodwin Watson. Washington, D.C.: National Training Laboratory, 1966.

Watts, Ross L. "Corporate Financial Statements, A Product of the Market and Political Processes." *Australian Journal of Management* (April 1977): 53-75.

Watts, Ross L., and Zimmerman, Jerold L. "The Demand for and Supply of Accounting Theories, The Market Excuses." *Accounting Review* (April 1979): 273-305.

Watts, Ross L., and Zimmerman, Jerold L. "Towards A Positive Theory of the Determination of Accounting Standards." *Accounting Review* (January 1978): 112-134.

Wyatt, Arthur. "The Economic Impact of Financial Accounting Standards." *Journal of Accountancy* (October 1977): 92–94.

Zaltman, Gerald, and Duncan, Robert. *Strategies for Planned Change.* New York: John Wiley & Sons, 1977.

Zeff, Stephen A. "The Rise of 'Economic Consequences.'" *Journal of Accountancy* (December 1978): 56–63.

Zeff, Stephen A. "Response: Comments on Accounting Principles—How They Are Developed." In *Institutional Issues in Public Accounting,* edited by Robert Sterling. Lawrence, Kansas: Scholars Book Co., 1973.

Zeff, Stephen A. *Forging Accounting Principles in Five Countries: A History and Analysis of Trends.* Champaign, Illinois: Stipes Publishing Company, 1972.

INDEX

Accounting research, role in policy making, 159–162
Accounting theory, role in policy making, 20–23, 158–159
Advisory Committee on Corporate Disclosure, 12–13
Agency theory of the firm, 23–24
APB, persuasive strategy, 74–77
Archibald, T. R., 117
Armstrong, Marshall, 31, 94
Arthur Young & Co., 134
Asebrook, Richard J., 100

Barlev, Benzion, 60, 128
Bastable, C. W., 134, 138
Beaver, William H., 117
Becker, Selwyn W., 117
Buckley, John W., 47
Burton, John C., 64
Business combinations, 76

Carmichael, D. R., 100
Carpenter, Charles G., 100, 135
Chandra, Gyan, 104
Change
  need for, 35–36, 106–108
  opposition to, 133–138
  resisting, 90
Change agent, 32
Change target, 32
Chatov, Robert, 65
Comiskey, Eugene E., 112, 139

Communication channels, 105–106
  APB, 39–40
  FASB, 40–42, 48–50
  SEC, 42–44
Compatibility, 98–100
Complexity, 100–102
Conformity
  attitudinal acceptance, 130–133
  behavioral compliance, 128–130
Cook, Ellen, 92, 100
Copeland, Ronald M., 111, 118
Corporate management
  interest in financial reporting, 29–30, 44–45, 98–100, 141–143
  role in disclosure system, 30–31
  role in policy making, 156–158
Corporate personality, 117–119
CPA, role in policy making, 155–156

Daily, R. Austin, 100, 135
Defliese, Philip L., 75
Dukes, Ronald E., 49

Economic consequences, 26–29, 30
  ex ante assessment, 45–47
  ex post analysis, 48–51
Evans, Thomas G., 48–49

FAF, 8
FASAC, 9

FASB
coercive strategy, 80
education/experimentation strategy, 77-80, 86
legitimate power, 57-61, 61-62
organization, 8-9
orientation to policy making, 17-18, 33
procedures, 9-10
pronouncements, 9-10
relationship with SEC, 58-59, 62-65

Flamholtz, Eric, 92, 100
Folks, William R., Jr., 48-49
Forecasting, 82-83, 99-100
Functional fixation, 116

Gagnon, J. M., 62, 112
Garsombke, H. Perrin, 134-135
Gellein, Oscar S., 15-16, 28-29
Gerboth, Dale L., 22-23, 27, 102
Goldman, Arien, 60, 128
Goshay, Robert C., 49
Greenball, Melvin N., 104
Groves, R. E., 112, 139

Hicks, James O., Jr., 107
Hepworth, S. R., 115
Hornbostel, Charles G., 36-37
Horngren, Charles T., 3, 27, 63, 73, 135
Hussein, Mohamed E. A., 113

Ijiri, Yuji, 116
Income smoothing, 115-116
Inflation accounting, 68-71, 77-80, 83-85, 97-98, 103-104, 126-128, 134-135
Information inductance, 46, 94, 133
Innovation decision studies
  accelerated depreciation, 110
  business combinations, 112
  inflation accounting, 113-114, 114-115
  installment reporting, 112-113
  LIFO, 110, 111
  revaluation of assets, 109-110

Innovation decisions
  authority, 122-123, 124-128
  collective, 122
  optional, 121
  over time, 138-140
  process, 120-121
  types of, 121-124
Innovation dissonance, 131-133
Innovations, 33-34
  characteristics of, 91, 93-105, 109-115
  criticism of, 133-135
  perceptions of, 91-93
Investment tax credit, 74-75

Jaedicke, Robert, 116
Jensen, Michael C., 23, 29
Jilling, Michael, 48-49

Kelly-Newton, Lauren, 114, 134
Kirk, Donald, J., 16
Knight, Kenneth, 116

Learning set, 116-117
Livingstone, John Leslie, 116

Marketable securities, 80-81
Mayer-Sommer, Alan P., 96
Meckling, William H., 23
Moonitz, Maurice, 56, 60-61, 74, 135

Nash, Manning, 111
Nichols, Donald, 60

Observability, 104-105
Oil and gas accounting, 65-68, 96-97

Peat, Marwick, Mitchell & Co., 49
Perceptions, 91-93, 106-107
Planned social change, 31-34
Policy maker
  challenges to, 135-138
  as change agent, 36-39
  role in policy making, 149-154
Policy making, 3
  model, 4-6, 143-149
  outside participation, 39-44
  political aspects, 26-27

positive theory of, 94–96
reporting economic reality orientation, 14
role of accounting research, 159–162
role of accounting theory, 20–23, 158–159
role of corporate management, 156–158
role of CPA, 155–156
role of FASB and SEC, 149–154
supplier orientation, 23–24
user orientation, 14–17
Prakash, Prem, 46, 133
Price, Kenneth, 60
Product-line reporting, 81–82, 96
Power bases, 53–54, 128–130
   AICPA, 56–57
   erosion of, 135–138
   FASB, 57–61, 61–62
   FASB and SEC interrelations, 62–65, 135–136
   FASB and SEC power struggles, 65–71
   SEC, 54–56, 62
   structural conditions, 61

Rappaport, Alfred, 46, 47, 63–64, 133
Regulation, 1–3
Relative advantage, 93–98
   observability of, 104–105
Rogers, Everett M., 93, 131
Ronen, Joshua, 115

Sadan, Simcha, 115
Savoie, Leonard M., 137
SEC
   coercive power, 54–56, 62
   coercive strategy, 84–85
   education/experimentation strategy, 81–84, 86–88
   organization, 10–11
   orientation to policy making, 19–20, 33
   persuasive strategy, 80–81
   procedures, 11–13
   pronouncements, 11
   relationship with FASB, 62–65
Shank, John K., 111, 118
Shoemaker, F. Floyd, 93, 131
Skousen, K. Fred, 81
Snow, Charles, 115
Social system effects, 106–108
Socio-political framework, 3–4, 141–143
   elements of, 34–51
Solomons, David, 16–17, 97–98
Sorter, George H., 117
Sterling, Robert R., 91
Strategies, 72–74
   APB, 74–77
   FASB, 77–80, 85–86
   SEC, 80–85, 86–88

Trialability, 102–104
Tritschler, Charles A., 109

U.S. House Subcommittee on Oversight & Investigation, 37
U.S. Senate Subcommittee on Governmental Efficiency and the District of Columbia, 38
U.S. Senate Subcommittee on Reports, Accounting and Management, 37–38

Warren, Donald, I., 61
Watts, Ross L., 21–22, 23, 30, 94–95
Williams, Harold, 69–70, 151–152
Wyatt, Arthur, 76

Zeff, Stephen A., 20–21, 27–28, 56, 74, 81
Zimmerman, Jerold, L., 21–22, 30, 94–95

LIBRARY OF DAVIDSON COLLEGE

Books on regular loan may be checked out for **two weeks**. Books must be presented at the Circulation Desk in order to be renewed.

A fine is charged after date due.

Special books are subject to special regulations at the discretion of the library staff.